GOLFING ON THE
ROOF OF THE WORLD

GOLFING ON THE ROOF OF THE WORLD

In Pursuit of
Gross National Happiness

Rick Lipsey

BLOOMSBURY

Published by Bloomsbury USA, New York
Distributed to the trade by Holtzbrinck Publishers

All papers used by Bloomsbury USA are natural, recyclable products made from wood grown in well-managed forests. The manufacturing processes conform to the environmental regulations of the country of origin.

LIBRARY OF CONGRESS CATALOGING-IN-PUBLICATION DATA HAS BEEN APPLIED FOR.

ISBN-10 1-59691-050-X
ISBN-13 978-1-59691-050-8

First U.S. Edition 2007

1 3 5 7 9 10 8 6 4 2

Typeset by Westchester Book Group
Printed in the United States of America by Quebecor World Fairfield

For the kids in Bhutan—my great inspiration

Happiness is spiritual, born of
Truth and Love.
—MARY BAKER EDDY

CONTENTS

CONTENTS

AUTHOR'S NOTE

The naming system in Bhutan is different from that used in most other societies. A few weeks after birth, babies are typically named by an abbot, who consults astrological scriptures and divination to determine an appropriate name. Names give no indication of sex. For example, I know many men named Dorji and many women named Dorji. In the past most Bhutanese had one-word names, but two-word names have become increasingly common, in part because so many Bhutanese have had problems abroad with customs officials. As for family names, only the royal family and a few other prominent families had them in the past. In recent years, more Bhutanese in the general population have begun using a parent's name as the family name. Women keep their names after marrying and don't inherit their husband's names, and children often have names with no connection to their parents' names. Some people have honorific titles, such as *lyonpo* or *dasho*, in front of their names, especially those who have been granted the honor of a special colored *kamney*, or scarf, by the king. Somebody with an orange scarf, including ministers and the chief justice, is a lyonpo, while somebody with a red scarf, the next most prestigious color, is a dasho.

Chapter 1

WOULD YOU LIKE TO BE OUR PRO?

I DIDN'T GO to Bhutan to play golf. Really. I went because of my wife.

Carrie and I love the outdoors and have done lots of hiking and backpacking, so before our wedding in 1995, I convinced her to let us honeymoon in the Himalayas. We spent a few days in Kathmandu and then flew to Pokhara, in central Nepal, about 75 miles northwest of Kathmandu, and embarked on an eight-day trek into the Annapurna Sanctuary. (The honeymoon also included four days on Samal Island in the Philippines, a detour Carrie demanded in exchange for the trek.)

On our honeymoon, we fell in love with the Himalayas, smitten by the beauty; the Buddhist and Hindu cultures; and the people, who had an attractive blend of tranquillity, kindness, and worldliness. During that trip, several travelers told us that Bhutan, a kingdom only 50 miles east of Nepal, was the hidden and unspoiled gem of the Himalayas, so we decided that our next Asian jaunt would be to Bhutan.

That's what led us in the spring of 2000 to plan a trip to Bhutan. We were really going to enjoy the scenery and rich culture, but while planning I looked to see whether they played golf in the world's last Buddhist kingdom. I'm always curious to see the odd places to which golf has migrated and to play the off-beat tracks. Such investigating has led me to unforgettable rounds in a high mountain valley in the Indian part of Kashmir and on a course wedged between two runways at the old Don Muang Airport in Bangkok, Thailand. Also, I knew that if there was golf in Bhutan my boss at *Sports Illustrated*, where I've been a staff golf writer since 1994, would want a story. Translation: free trip.

In the course of my research, I sent an e-mail to the Bhutan Tourism Corporation (BTC), which handled all tourism in the kingdom until the industry was privatized in 1991. I wrote: "Hello. I'm an American seeking a recommendation of a tour operator to organize a trip. My wife and I want to see your culture, trek and play golf."

A few days later, my in-box had a message labeled *GOLF IN BHUTAN*. It was from Sonam Wangchuk Kesang, a Bhutanese from Thimphu, the capital city. He was leaving a job at the BTC and starting his own tour company. He told me that he was a keen golfer; that Royal Thimphu was one of the world's highest courses; and that he was an 8-handicapper and the Bhutanese king was a 13-handicapper. He ended by writing, "If you wish to play and arrange a tour to Bhutan, I am most happy to assist you."

I felt like a lottery winner. Over the next few weeks, Sonam Kesang and I traded correspondence and began a friendship based on our mutual passion for golf. I peppered Sonam Kesang with questions about golf in Bhutan, trekking, and Bhutanese cuisine. Sonam Kesang asked me just one question: "Can you bring me new clubs and golf clothes?"

When I asked why, Sonam Kesang gave two reasons. First,

there are no golf shops in Bhutan, and the handful of tiny sporting goods shops in Thimphu don't sell golf equipment because the market is minuscule. So Bhutanese golfers buy equipment and apparel when traveling abroad; they have friends bring it into Bhutan; or they purchase used models. Second, Sonam Kesang could have bought stuff over the Internet, but shipping it to Bhutan was a logistical nightmare and outrageously expensive.

Sonam Kesang explained the problem in an e-mail. A couple of years earlier, he'd ordered golf clubs from an online retailer based in the U.S., and the store told him that they would send them to Bhutan by FedEx. But the clubs got stuck in Dubai. "I discovered the hard way that FedEx does not, as they claim, ship 'anytime, anywhere.' Rather, they ship, 'anytime, anywhere. But not to Bhutan.'" Sonam Kesang then learned that DHL shipped to Bhutan, but the fee would have been a few hundred dollars and Sonam Kesang would have also been required to pay a huge import tax. "So I gave up," he wrote.

In his e-mail, Sonam Kesang told me exactly what he wanted—a Big Bertha Steelhead driver, 3-wood, and 5-wood; two Odyssey putters; and a set of X-12 Callaway irons. He also provided exact specifications for shaft types and loft and lie settings, and even more astounding, he told me where to get the gear.

Sonam Kesang directed me to the World of Golf, a store on East 47th Street in Manhattan, and told me to ask for the 5-percent Bhutan discount. He also asked me to go to Niketown, on 57th Street just off Fifth Avenue, and get five golf shirts. "I prefer red and blue," he wrote.

The e-mails sounded preposterous, like those get-rich-quick missives from Nigerian businessmen. I wondered whether Sonam Kesang was suckering me, but I was intrigued and had already wired him several thousand dollars as payment for our tour, so I figured I had to trust him, and I followed his directions. While driving across Manhattan to the World of Golf, I wondered whether the salesman was going to think I was crazy by asking for the Bhutan discount. The salesman, however, didn't even laugh. He took my order as if it were perfectly normal. "We enjoy doing business with our Bhutanese customers," he said.

FAST FORWARD TO October 2000. We arrived in Bhutan after four flights over two days and more angst than I'd ever experienced on a vacation. The problem was that you rarely get plane tickets for a trip to Bhutan in advance. First, Bhutan's national airline, Druk Air, doesn't have electronic ticketing. Also, the tour companies ship the paper tickets to the Druk Air office in the city from which you're flying into the kingdom, which in our case was Bangkok, so you don't get the tickets until you check in for the flight. Several Americans who'd been to Bhutan told us that they, too, didn't believe the archaic system would work, and feared being stranded in the airport—Bangkok, Calcutta, Delhi, and Kathmandu are the main gateways—and losing the thousands of dollars they'd wired to the tour operator. But the system works, although your heart thumps until the very last minute.

Soon after arriving in Bhutan, Carrie and I were soaking up the glorious panorama while standing on the first tee at the Royal Thimphu Golf Club in Thimphu, which has nine holes and two sets of tees for those who want to play eighteen. The course is 2,700 yards long. I've played a lot of golf. I've played the holes hard by the Pacific Ocean at Pebble Beach and in Amen Corner at Augusta National. The sights and sounds here, though, were unlike anything I'd experienced on a golf course.

In one sense, the atmosphere was otherworldly and distinctly Himalayan. There were eagles soaring overhead and cavernous and lushly wooded mountains rising vertically to the sky around us. Horns from monks praying at a nearby monastery were blaring. The course was next to the gargantuan Thimphu *dzong*, a fortlike structure housing Bhutan's top government and religious officials. As we stood on the tee at the 100-yard downhill par-3 first hole, gleaming right ahead of us and less than 100 yards behind the green was a golden spire atop a regal-looking building that resembled a big monastery.

There were also some amusing Bhutanese touches. One was a local rule printed on the scorecard: "A ball lying within one club length around the tree, can be dropped without penalty, no closer to the hole. If the golfer plays and hits the tree with his/her club, the player will automatically be disqualified." Protecting the natural environment is a key facet of Buddhism, which is the foundation of Bhutanese culture and the state religion, but I never expected to see the Buddhist mores in force at the golf course. I also heard men in the clubhouse talking about a tournament that is definitely unique to Bhutan: the Yak Open. The event, held every couple of years at Royal Thimphu, awards parts of a yak—raw and unskinned—to the winners. "The legs have the juiciest meat, so they go to the first-place man," a golfer told me.

But the atmosphere also, strangely, felt like any other course in the world, and that was comforting. Guys coming off the last green were settling bets. On the clubhouse steps, Sonam Kesang and his friends were talking about when their regular foursome would tee off on Saturday. A player on the first tee duffed his tee shot into the tiny pond in front of the green, and his partners began ribbing him while the caddies chuckled.

When we were teeing off at the first, Sonam Kesang suggested that I aim at the golden spire.

"Do monks live there?" I asked.

"It's not a monastery," Sonam Kesang said. "It's the High Court."

Carrie, a lawyer, perked up. "Aim at that," she said excitedly.

While Carrie and I were awestruck with the scenery, Sonam Kesang was unfazed, apparently immune to the jaw-dropping setting, much like I don't blink when I see the Empire State Building or the reservoir in Central Park. We were also confused by the altitude (Thimphu is 7,500 feet above sea level). I'd never played golf above sea level, so I was unsure how much farther my ball would fly.

"About one club extra," said Karma (Randy) Rangdol, the fourth person in our group.

A six-time Bhutan Open champion and a 3-handicapper, Randy was forty-six years old and the managing director of the Bhutan Development Finance Corporation. Randy is diminutive (5'5", 130 pounds), but he has Popeye forearms and palms calloused from hitting so many golf balls. He also has a long, syrupy swing that produces prodigious distance, especially with a driver. "They call me Shorty Woods," Randy said. His cheeks are soft and round. His brown eyes, always wide open, are unusually large for his small face. He has a raspy, high-pitched voice. "I usually hit a little wedge on this hole," Randy said.

On Randy's advice, I asked for a wedge from my caddie. In the States, caddies routinely carry two bags per round, but in Bhutan each player has his own caddie, and the caddies never carry the bags. Instead, the golfers all have pull carts, and the caddies simply maneuver the carts around the course. The caddies are lanky boys ranging in age from ten to sixteen. Most of the regular loopers at Royal Thimphu come from poor families and go to school, but some of the boys are dropouts. I've always wondered why the Royal Thimphu members permit such young boys to caddie on weekdays, when they know the kids should be at school. Some members have told me that the club is working on the problem, while others have said the caddies would not go to school even if the club didn't let them caddie and that instead the boys would either sit at home or perhaps get into trouble.

The boy working for me was fifteen and slender. He said he was in school, but we were playing on a weekday, so I doubt he was telling the truth. He was wearing flip-flops and a *gho*, a knee-length robe belted at the waist that's the national dress for men. At my home course, Westchester Country Club, he'd have looked like an extra from *The Last Emperor*. Here he looked entirely natural. He pulled the wedge from the pull cart and handed it to me with a smile.

With full confidence, I waggled a little to loosen up, drew back the wedge, and swung. The ball sailed out into the thin Himalayan air, out over the green, and landed in a swale. So far, the American contingent was making a poor showing. Carrie would have to redeem us.

She lifted a 9-iron, and Randy and Sonam Kesang gasped.

"My gosh! A lefty!" Randy shrieked.

Carrie is used to hearing jokes about being a left-handed golfer, so she just shrugged. "I hope I make contact," she said while taking a practice swing.

Randy and Sonam Kesang were shocked not just because Carrie was a left-hander, but also because she was a woman. That combination, they said, had never occurred at Royal

Thimphu. The historic first shot by a left-handed woman on Bhutanese soil wasn't pretty: a low skull, almost a shank, which ricocheted left and into some bushes.

Carrie was unfazed. "Should I hit another?" she said.

"As you like," said Randy, chuckling.

Carrie's second shot was a dribbler that trickled down the hill to the front of the green. "Welcome to Bhutan," said Randy while walking down the hill.

Sonam Kesang was wearing some of the clothes that I'd brought him from Niketown: a blue shirt, khaki pants, white golf shoes, and a blue baseball cap. I don't know where Sonam Kesang got his Oakley wraparound sunglasses, but it wasn't in Bhutan. You can only buy fake sunglasses there. His outfit was like what David Duval used to wear, and Sonam Kesang also had a goatee like Duval's. I asked if the resemblance to the 2001 British Open champion was a coincidence. "Not at all," Sonam Kesang said. "Mr. Duval is my favorite player. When I dress like Mr. Duval, I feel better, like I'm going to play great."

After just one hole, the aura of the surroundings was already fading, replaced by the similarities in mannerisms and mentality between Bhutanese golfers and golfers back home. I was quickly learning why golfers everywhere relate to each other so well. Those who play the game may do so in different physical settings and come from starkly different cultures, but on the course the barriers disappear because everybody feels a bond and is on the same wavelength—one that transcends skin color, sex, and age.

Royal Thimphu was lush with verdant fairways and greens, a surprise because it was early fall and the course didn't have a sprinkler system. "How do you water the course?" I asked on the second tee.

Sonam Kesang pointed his driver at the blue sky. He explained that the course remained green and soft until mid-October because the monsoon season usually extends until the middle of September and there is plenty of runoff after that. By early fall, the temperatures begin to cool, dropping into the low sixties during the day, and it hardly rains again until late the following spring, so the grass begins to wither and the fairways become rock hard. "We used to try to fertilize the course in winter to keep it green and playable," Sonam Kesang said. "But that didn't work. The only fertilizer we could get was cow manure, but that brought up cloves, so we gave up. Now we just don't play in January and February."

After hitting a drive onto the second fairway, Sonam Kesang asked me if his grip was correct.

"Take another shot," I said. "Let me watch more closely."

The second hole is a slightly uphill 420-yard par 4 with a slight bend from left to right. I studied Sonam Kesang's swing and noticed that he was abruptly lifting his club during the backswing. So on the tee at the third hole, a 500-yard downhill par 5, I stood a few feet behind him and crouched like a baseball catcher, figuring that he'd know about American baseball. He did. "You need a mask and a mitt," Sonam Kesang said.

"Just pretend I'm wearing a mitt," I said. "Try sweeping the club back low and slow so your clubhead hits my imaginary mitt."

Sonam Kesang did what I said and launched a towering drive down the fairway. That elicited a smile. "We need a real coach and a real driving range," he said.

After I hit, I looked back to the other tee on the hole. A woman, weather-beaten with deeply tanned and wrinkled skin, was on her hands and knees clipping grass around the edge of the tee with scissors. I wasn't shocked. Yes, it was drastically different from how courses are maintained in the States, but I'd seen this primitive form of course manicuring in Nepal, so this wasn't new to me.

I also hit a good drive, leaving myself in the fairway with 200 yards to the green. I hit a 2-iron but caught it a little thin, and the ball landed 30 yards short of the green and rolled into the pond in front of the green. When we reached the pond, a few boys were swimming in the dank water. One of the boys, a skinny but muscular kid who appeared to be about ten, waded over to the side. He leaned against the edge and stretched his arms out on the grass. I looked down and his little hands were cupped. Inside he held my ball, a white Pinnacle, shimmering like a pearl in an oyster.

The boy looked me in the eyes. He was stone-faced. "Twenty-five ngultrums," he said.

That was cheap to me. In the Bhutanese currency, whose rate is tied directly to the Indian rupee, one ngultrum is worth about two cents. But still, my cheeks were red. Sonam Kesang and Randy were standing on the green and laughing. Meanwhile, Carrie was oblivious to the comedic interlude because she and her caddie were scrounging for her ball in the rough behind the green. I had no choice. I swallowed my pride and handed the kid twenty-five ngultrums.

I was surprised that neither Randy nor Sonam Kesang intervened on my behalf. But while we were putting, Sonam Kesang said, "Happens all the time. Our kids are capitalists."

I laughed. It was amusing to see that caddies everywhere have the same mischievous mentality. I know about that, because I spent a decade during high school and college looping at clubs in Westchester County. We routinely took advantage of the golfers, throwing their balls into the woods if the bags were too heavy and turning bad lies into good ones to make the players happy and speed the pace of play.

The tee at no. 5, a 320-yard dogleg left par 4, points directly at the Thimphu dzong, which is about 600 yards away. "Aim at the office in the top right corner of the dzong," said Randy. "It's the king's office."

"Is he there now?" Carrie asked.

"No," Randy said. "When he's in, the windows are open."

"Do animals from the hills ever get onto the course?" I asked.

Randy laughed. "Big problem," he said. "Development has taken away all the grazing space in Thimphu, so the farmers like to bring their cows to graze here. It's a constant battle."

"I was thinking more serious stuff, like tigers or lions," I said.

More laughter from Randy. "We've seen Himalayan black bears, but nobody's been attacked," he said.

The tee at no. 8, a downhill 200-yard par 3, is bordered to the right by a well-trafficked paved road with a sidewalk. A chain-link fence separates the course from the road, and several passersby, mostly schoolchildren but a few elderly men and women, too, stopped to watch us tee off. The kids giggled, and the old people looked at us quizzically. Randy and Sonam Kesang paid them no attention. They were used to the distraction. I, though, was struck by the social juxtaposition. Only the upper class in Bhutan can afford to play golf, and Royal Thimphu is regarded by the hoi polloi as a playground for the upper crust. Here was another glaring similarity between golf in Bhutan and the game in America.

Walking along the fairway at our final hole, the 400-yard ninth, Sonam Kesang told me how he had gotten into golf. He grew up playing basketball and archery, and as a young adult focused on archery, the national sport, starring on a team that was a perennial contender for the national championship. He first learned about golf in the mid-1980s when he was at a friend's house in Thimphu and saw his friend's father hitting balls into a net in front of a mirror. "I thought the man was crazy and that golf was a silly game," said Sonam Kesang.

A decade later, somebody offered to give Sonam Kesang an old set of clubs. "I took them grudgingly," he said. "As an athlete, though, I figured I had to at least give the game a try. I did and was immediately hooked."

GOLF ARRIVED IN Bhutan in the mid-1970s, in the person of a young man named Benji Dorji. Benji is part of one of the kingdom's most prominent families (his father was the first prime minister), and from 1974 to 1987 he was the country's first chief justice. He developed a passion for the game during frequent vacations to Calcutta, India, first with his family as a child and later as an adult. But Benji never had anywhere to play upon returning to Bhutan.

In Thimphu, he finally found an ally: an Indian Army general named Jaganathan, who had been a friend of his father's. Jaganathan had been brought to Bhutan to help supervise the building of the first paved roads, and later became the commander of IMTRAT, the Indian Military Training Team, which since the early 1950s has worked in Bhutan to oversee development of the Bhutanese Army and to implement major infrastructure projects such as roads and bridges. Jaganathan was a keen golfer, too, and with Benji's encouragement, they suggested to the king that if they were allowed to build a course on the unused farmland adjacent the dzong, it would forever preserve the green open space. The king told them, "You're crazy, chaps. But you can have the land."

The course, built by Indian soldiers, was rough, and the greens were made of sand with oil burned into them, a common practice at courses where the weather is harsh or budgets are small. The handful of people who played the course, including Jaganathan and Benji, carried doormats to hit off. Gradually the game gained a foothold, although there were still only about a dozen players by the end of the seventies. The king was an avid athlete, and after some time he asked Benji "to help me play this stupid game."

OUR ROUND ENDED with a flourish. At the final hole, I made a 2-putt par and Carrie drained a 6-footer for a 6. "Can we play tomorrow?" Carrie asked.

"I'm not sure if they'll let you back," I said. "Not after that display on the first tee."

"Unfortunately, you're heading off to Paro tomorrow morning," Sonam Kesang said. "This round will have to suffice."

AFTER THE ROUND, I visited Chang Tshering, the course superintendent, in his office, a rickety wood hut near the clubhouse. Cobwebs hung from musty rafters, and Tshering worked from a decrepit wood desk with nothing more than a yellowed computer. "It's never worked," said Tshering. "Or maybe it does work, but not for me. I don't know about computers."

Tshering, twenty-eight, had a gentle presence. Rail thin and 5'10", he had an indelible smile and wore a black baseball hat with the Royal Thimphu Golf Club logo, a circular patch with the club's name written around a jagged snowcapped mountain.

I was interested to learn about the logistics of maintaining a golf course in Bhutan.

"Why do people trim grass with scissors?" I asked.

"We have just one mowing machine," said Tshering. "But it usually breaks, and we have to order parts from Japan. That takes many weeks. We must have the grass trimmed, or people will complain. My staff works very hard."

The course operated on a shoestring budget, but Tshering and his staff seemed to handle it with grace and good spirits. The hardest part, he said, was the cows. "Their footprints go everywhere. They like greens. And their pee has poison acid that kills turf. That's why we have brown spots in many places on the roughs and fairways. And with the cows come the farmers who graze them, and those farmers steal our bunker rakes."

Tshering stood, grabbed a wedge, took a golf stance, and began waggling the club. "How should I address the ball with my driver?" he said.

"Why do you ask me?" I replied.

"I saw you giving help to Mr. Kesang and Mr. Rangdol," Tshering said. "You must be a teacher."

"I think you should move the ball forward in your stance," I said. "Also try to hit the inside quadrant of the ball."

Tshering and I went outside so he could take a couple of practice swings. After them, he looked up, smiling. "You are a good coach," he said.

As AFTERNOON DRIFTED into evening and the sun dipped below the mountains, Sonam Kesang and Randy invited us to join them for drinks and snacks in the clubhouse. Except for the pack of dogs patrolling the parking lot, the one-room building resembled a monastery, with its pagoda-shaped roof and walls festooned with colorful Buddhist motifs. Inside, the dining area was sparsely decorated: a concrete floor, a few rectangular wooden tables, and lots of wooden folding chairs. The walls were covered with large pinewood plaques listing the winners of the club's tournaments. A large photograph of the king had pride of place on the far wall, as it did in literally every establishment in the kingdom, from homes to restaurants to bars to offices to gas stations.

The atmosphere inside felt the same as I've experienced in clubhouses outside of Bhutan. Guys in polo shirts and khaki pants drank beer and smoked cigarettes and cigars while bantering about bad shots, big bets, newfangled equipment, and all things Tiger. (In subsequent trips, a hot topic of conversation was whether Tiger should have married a Swedish nanny. The verdict: a resounding yes.) When a member wanted something, he'd call one of the female attendants, who would sheepishly arrive a couple of minutes later with the food or beverage. The vast economic and social schism at Royal Thimphu between golfers and club staff, though, was not jarring, because I've seen it at clubs all over the world.

My mind was whirring like a prayer wheel. I was in Bhutan, as different and as far away from New York as I could be. I hadn't known anybody for more than a couple of days. Yet I felt comfortable and content, like I was at home. In the clubhouse, we sat around a table. Sonam Kesang ordered fried pork *mo mos* (a type of dumpling) and fried rice.

"We had a blast today," I said.

Sonam Kesang smiled. "Does your work at *Sports Illustrated* permit you to leave for a long time?" he said.

"We get four weeks of vacation every year," I said.

Sonam Kesang smiled. "What would you think about being our golf pro?" he asked.

"We really need help," Randy said.

I laughed. Carrie was laughing, too. Sonam Kesang had to be joking. "Rick would ruin your games," said Carrie.

Sonam Kesang, though, wasn't laughing. "We'd like to have you return and work for us," Sonam Kesang said.

I laughed again. This time, however, my laugh wasn't relaxed and free. It was tense and nervous. Sonam Kesang's serious look was unnerving. I knew something was brewing, but I couldn't fathom it. I didn't know what to say. "Sure," I replied.

I expected Sonam Kesang to crack a smile and end the joke. He didn't.

"We've never had a real teacher," said Sonam Kesang. "All we know about the swing comes from videos and magazines people bring back from trips."

"You'll be our David Leadbetter," said Randy.

Randy was laughing. But Sonam Kesang still was not.

If the Bhutanese are anything, it is blunt and honest. There's not a comedian in the country.

What was happening? Could we move to Bhutan? Could I come alone and leave Carrie behind? Would *Sports Illustrated* grant me a sabbatical? Was I qualified to teach a kingdom how to play golf? What would I do about my mother, who was back at home and had recently been diagnosed with cancer? What about my grandmother? I was in charge of her affairs. Who would take care of our cats, Max and Nala? Carrie had been talking about wanting to start a family. Could we do it in Bhutan?

I looked at Carrie.

"You're not seriously thinking about this, are you?" Carrie said.

Things seemed to be happening in slow motion. The smoke

and yapping that filled the clubhouse had become dreamy background music.

"Yes, I'll come," I said. "When do you want me?"

BACK IN THE richer sea-level air of Manhattan, I thought a little more carefully about what I'd agreed to. Bhutan is literally on the other side of the earth from New York. A tiny nation covering 18,147 square miles—about twice the size of New Jersey—the kingdom has no stoplights, escalators, or chain stores. There are two elevators, one swimming pool (which has been empty and broken for years), and a single airport with one runway. Buddhism pervades every aspect of the country's life and culture. Having multiple spouses is not common but it is legal, and the king himself has four wives, all of them sisters. (The queens have a fifth sister whom the king didn't marry.)

Bhutan is at a crossroads, perhaps the most critical juncture in its history. The country had virtually closed its doors to foreigners until the early 1970s, but it is now embarking on a grand experiment with potentially terrific or terrible consequences as it tries to become a global citizen. In doing that, Bhutan wants to simultaneously embrace the future (technology, modernity, and commerce) and the past (ancient Buddhist cultural customs and mores).

Perhaps the biggest change involves the government. In the mid-1990s, King Jigme Singye Wangchuck, the fourth monarch in Bhutan's history, decided that Bhutan couldn't survive as an isolated monarchy and should transform into a constitutional democracy run by officials elected by the people. (The first elections are scheduled for 2008, and the new constitution will likely be enacted shortly thereafter.) That would turn the king into mainly a symbolic leader, much like Queen Elizabeth in England. The king had several reasons for wanting the change. The most prominent could have been Bhutan's Himalayan neighbor Nepal, which had endured decades of instability, including royal-family assassinations, failed attempts at creating a democracy, Maoist insurgencies, and environmental devastation. Also, internecine feuds, love trysts, and cronyism nearly destroyed Bhutan's royal family and its kingdom when the king was a child in the 1960s and early '70s, and perhaps he understood that it might be only a matter of time until a similar situation could again imperil the nation.

Ironically, most Bhutanese vehemently disagree with the king and think his changes could turn Bhutan into another Nepal, or worse. That negative attitude has been widely proffered in the fledgling world of Bhutanese blogging. Here's one posting from the readers' forum at *kuenselonline.com*:

> Heaven is nowhere on earth except Bhutan, but far behind the curtain I have lots of doubts.... Corruption will definitely remain as the most dangerous issue.... We have perhaps the only distinct culture ever surviving in the world, but day by day I find it disappearing.... As a citizen, I have a worry.—CDORSHA

All the change seems to be having mixed results. Bhutan legalized the Internet and TV in 1999, but they've since had a dramatic rise in youth crime that some Bhutanese officials believe is directly related to violent programs children watch. (To help stem the surge in youth violence, the cable station that aired pro wrestling was banned in 2005.) Disposable diapers are fast replacing cloth ones, at least in Thimphu, but Pampers and other disposable products have contributed to the fast rise in litter, as witnessed in the garbage-infested streams in Thimphu. Other relatively recent and unwelcome problems include drunken fights outside nightclubs, poor construction workers from Bangladesh and India living in shantytowns, and Bhutanese Christians holding worship services in living rooms because they claim the government won't let them build churches. Also, the government was recently forced to create an anticorruption commission to deal with the surfeit of illicit activity in the private and public sectors.

But Bhutan remains an anomaly in South Asia because it has never been colonized and has also made huge gains in education, the economy, and health care. Per capita income is $770 annually, which is $180 above the average for South Asian countries. The school system has mushroomed from 11 schools and a few hundred students in 1961 to more than 450 schools and a university (in all of which courses are taught in English, not the national language, Dzongkha), catering to over 160,000 students. And the average life expectancy has skyrocketed from 49 to 66 over the past 15 years. All of these factors have helped make the Bhutanese astonishingly happy and relaxed. Just talking to a Bhutanese is like getting a massage; the slow and rhythmic cadence of their voices and the gentle aura of their presence have remarkably calming effects.

That is surely the result, at least partly, of the kingdom's unique policy, gross national happiness (GNH). What's that? Governments typically measure prosperity by gross domestic product, but not Bhutan. The king created GNH shortly after ascending to the throne in 1972, at age seventeen, to help his people strive more for the spiritual virtues espoused by Buddhism than materialism, which he knew would be a huge challenge as Bhutan modernized.

GNH isn't rooted in numbers. It's a holistic principle, which, if adhered to, is supposed to help people develop their lives happily on individual and collective bases. GNH doesn't have a how-to manual or a set of guidelines; it has four things that people are asked to dedicate themselves to promoting: sustainable and equitable socioeconomic development; environmental conservation; cultural preservation; and good governance in the form of democracy.

Since His Majesty introduced it, GNH has been embraced not only by the Bhutanese, but it's also gained significant currency far beyond the Himalayas. For example, senior politicians in Canada, Thailand, and Great Britain have begun developing well-being indexes based on GNH, and, starting in 2004, annual GNH conferences have been attended by hundreds of prominent scholars, government officials, businesspeople, and writers from around the world.

With GNH and the rest of its unique characteristics, Bhutan was utterly different, and I wanted to live there.

SONAM KESANG AND I set to work on a proposal to present to the Royal Thimphu members to convince them to hire me as their first teaching professional. I promised to provide expert instruction, start a junior golf program, and solicit equipment donations from my contacts at sporting goods companies to use in my teaching and later donate to the club so they'd have nice equipment for guests. In exchange, I asked the club to pay travel and living expenses for Carrie and me, but I didn't request a salary. It took half a year for Sonam Kesang, who was the secretary at

Royal Thimphu, to convince the members to invite me, but he got the okay in March 2001 for me to come that fall. I agreed to stay for three months. Carrie and I feverishly began planning, until a bombshell dropped on us a few weeks later: Carrie was pregnant, and her due date was in early January 2002.

That meant we couldn't go to Bhutan in the fall of 2001. I was nervous that Royal Thimphu wouldn't let me delay the program for a year, and Sonam Kesang wasn't sure he'd be able to convince the membership. So I was literally jumping for joy when I got an e-mail from Sonam Kesang that said we could come in the fall of 2002, and even better, the club would be glad to pay for our baby's airfare.

After our general plans were confirmed, Carrie began looking for something to do in Bhutan. With dogged research and exceptional karma, she found work as a special consultant to Bhutan's chief justice. Carrie's assignment was not nearly as glamorous as my gig, at least in the eyes of my golf buddies, but it was infinitely more important. Claudia, our newborn, also had big goals for our time in Bhutan: taking her first steps (assisted) and saying her first words.

AFTER ONE LAST whirlwind round of packing and negotiation ("You're taking my granddaughter to Bhutan over my dead body!" may well have been my mother-in-law's last words before we departed), we left JFK, circling the lights of the Big Apple once before heading to the Himalayas.

It was September 2002. We were cruising at 32,000 feet on a Druk Air flight from Bangkok to Paro, about 25 miles west of Thimphu, the tip of my nose rubbing against the airplane window. The glistening snow-white Himalayan peaks rested peacefully against the bright blue sky, and the panorama seemed fake, like a poster.

The Himalayas stretch in a 1,300-mile crescent through the Indian subcontinent. Passing through five countries—Bhutan, India, Nepal, Pakistan, and Tibet—they're an utterly remote mass of snow and rock that starts at sea level and rises higher than any place on earth, with nine of the ten tallest mountains, including Everest, in Nepal and Tibet, and the highest unclimbed peak, Gangkar Punsum, in Bhutan. (The Bhutanese government forbids mountain climbing out of respect for the traditional religious significance of the peaks, which are considered deities, and to avoid disrupting mountain villagers.)

The Himalayas are home to a wildly rich array of ecosystems, although much of the flora and fauna in Nepal have been desecrated. But Bhutan is perhaps the world's most environmentally sensitive nation, which is why its habitats are immaculately preserved. In Bhutan, for example, more than forty-five species of rhododendrons exist and bloom every spring; snow leopards roam freely (sightings are rare, although a friend came face-to-face with a regular leopard); rare and endangered black-necked cranes migrate south from China and Tibet to spend the winter in the Phobjikha Valley; and naturalists have found at least three hundred species of mushroom, including the delicious matsutake, which can sell for more than $100 a pound in Japan.

The Himalayas are also home to dozens of indigenous cultures, many of which live as they did centuries ago, without electricity, running water, or virtually any other modern comfort. Perhaps surprisingly, the Himalayas are also home to a small but growing group of chic folks who are as wired, stylish, and educated as people from Bangalore and Los Angeles, and it's within this clan of Himalayan dwellers that golf is gaining a small foothold.

That's why the Himalayas are now home to a few dozen golf courses of varying size and quality. The plush ones include the Gokarna Forest Resort in Kathmandu, the capital of Nepal, and the Robert Trent Jones–designed Royal Springs Golf Course in Srinagar, the capital of the Indian-controlled part of Kashmir. In the middle of the spectrum is Royal Thimphu, which is akin to a solid municipal course in the United States. And at the low end are rough-hewn tracks on military bases throughout Bhutan.

The British Aerospace 146 jet in which we were flying was one of two planes owned by Druk Air, the only carrier with access to Bhutan. The pint-size jet carries seventy-six passengers and is powered by four massive Rolls-Royce engines that allow it to ascend and descend quickly and bank from side to side. You begin to appreciate the maneuverability when you look out the window while the pilot is navigating through the deep and twisty Himalayan valleys. The engines also provide an exceptionally smooth ride, which is good because Druk Air passengers usually spend as much time out of their seats as in them, as they shift from side to side to glimpse the jaw-dropping scenery.

Despite being six miles above sea level, we were only a mile or two above the thickly forested Bhutanese valleys, and every few minutes we'd fly over a farming community that seemed to be a million miles from anywhere.

The farms weren't like anything in America. Bhutanese farmers live in a world so vertical you can get vertigo just looking at it. Their farms are carved into mountainsides, with long, narrow, and rectangular fields that are often stacked like staircases. The farms grow crops including rice (some of it a distinctive red color), wheat, and potatoes, and the houses all look alike. About the size of a Dairy Queen, the homes are square, have three floors, and are built of mud, yak dung, and wood beams with slate roofs held in place by rocks. (Bhutanese tradition prohibits the use of man-made objects, including nails, in buildings.) Yaks pull wooden plows to turn over the soil. Ancient stone monasteries are surrounded by groves of blue, red, yellow, and green prayer flags on tall wooden poles.

In the twenty minutes from when we crossed the Indian border into southern Bhutan until we landed in Paro, I didn't see a single road and I wondered: How do the people visit friends? Shop? Transport goods to markets? Get mail? Do they have electricity? Telephones? A couple of hours earlier, I'd been in Bangkok, a bustling megalopolis, but now I was looking at an ancient culture straight out of the pages of *National Geographic.*

Even stranger, these were the people to whom I would soon be teaching golf. Well, that's an exaggeration. My primary mission wasn't to teach farmers and yak herders. Royal Thimphu is in Thimphu, a city whose population, including its sprawling suburbs, is nearly a hundred thousand, and which has modern conveniences including electricity, paved roads, and the Internet. It's even home to the nation's only female cabbie, Tshering Lhamo, who faced chauvinistic resistance when she began her career as a hack in 2006. "Even the traffic police stopped me several times to check if I had the required license," Lhamo recently told *Kuensel,* a weekly that was the kingdom's only newspaper until a second paper, the *Bhutan Times,* was launched in 2006.

Royal Thimphu's membership of one hundred is comprised of businessmen, senior government officials, and the royal family, because they are the only Bhutanese who can afford the $180 annual membership dues and the cost of equipment. The membership, which had risen fivefold over the past decade, had brought me to Bhutan primarily to lower their handicaps. But the members also wanted me to teach children from all socioeconomic backgrounds and try to bring golf to the kingdom's remote areas. The members (all but two were men) dreamed that the next Tiger Woods could be from Bhutan.

While I was full of anticipation on the flight, Carrie was asleep. Like her mother, Carrie had at first been against this trip. Surviving for months without dry cleaning, the *New York Times*, and Starbucks was unfathomable. Worse, bringing a baby to Bhutan was the epitome of idiocy. Gradually, however, Carrie warmed to the idea. Carrie, like me, is addicted to traveling, and this would be our third trip to the Himalayas and her fourth jaunt to Asia. Also, Carrie's job with the chief justice seemed thrilling, and not just for the chance to help shape the kingdom's legal system. The job allowed Carrie to work on her own schedule, leaving ample time to play golf, explore the kingdom, and frolic with Claudia. By the time we left New York, Carrie was as excited as I was.

So why, on the verge of arriving in Bhutan, was Carrie out cold? Carrie always sleeps at the beginning of big trips. It's her way of avoiding the rush of emotions that can overwhelm you at the outset of an adventure.

Meanwhile, Claudia was in the seat between Carrie and me, and our firstborn was also fast asleep. Buried in her car seat that was buckled into the plane seat, Claudia's little head was sagging over her right shoulder while a stream of drool was dribbling from one corner of her mouth. Was Claudia's mind also a whirl of anticipation? Did she understand where we were going? Was she sad that she wasn't going to see Grandma, Grandpa, or Great-Grandma for a long time? I'm not a mind reader, but I know this: Claudia, like Carrie, snores softly.

I often turned from the window to look at Claudia. I admired her billowy locks, her ruddy, round cheeks, and the gentle curves of her ears. Perhaps only a parent understands the feeling, but looking at a sleeping baby—*your* sleeping baby—incites a secure sense of joy and peace.

I was also filled with curiosity. How would the trip change Claudia? What would she remember about the Himalayas? Would she like Bhutan's sizzling chilies?

"Hello," the Druk Air captain serenely said as we began the descent. "We're a few minutes from landing. Don't be alarmed if the trees look very big and close to the plane. They *are*. But everything is fine. This is our normal approach."

We were closing in on the airport, a one-runway gem that's a do-it-right-the-first-time-or-die proposition wedged into a deep mountain valley. Amazingly, the airport has had only a few minor accidents—a flat tire and the tip of a wing scraping the runway are among them—and no fatalities since it opened in the early 1980s. But in midair, or whatever's lower than midair, this wasn't too comforting. The plane was so close to terra firma that I could make out individual tree branches and the horns on the yaks pulling plows.

Suddenly the plane banked to the left, back to the right, and then again to the left. My life is over, I thought. We made another hard turn and plunged over a ridge, threading between the steep valley walls toward the runway. I closed my eyes. After a buttery-soft landing, the jet reached the end of the runway, made a 180-degree turn, and taxied back to the terminal, which was like no terminal you've ever seen. The two-floor structure, like almost every building in Bhutan, resembles a monastery, its white walls festooned with ornate carvings of Buddhist motifs and the roof covered with thousands of pieces of slate.

While walking across the tarmac, I thought about *Golf in the Kingdom*, Michael Murphy's seminal golf novel from 1972 that depicts the game's mystical and magnetic qualities better than

anything ever written. I've read the best seller several times, starting in high school, and I've always wondered what it would be
like to play a round with Shivas Irons, the monklike golf pro who
is the book's main character, at Burningbush, the fictitious Scot-
tish links where the story unfolds. Unfortunately, that'll never
happen. But, I thought while holding Claudia and soaking up the
scene, this adventure will be the next best thing, because I'll be
playing and teaching golf in the last Buddhist kingdom.

Chapter 2

APPLE PIE AND BICHONS
FRISES AT BENJI'S

SONAM KESANG WAS waiting at the airport to pick us up. He had brought along a surprise: Tashi Wangchuk, our tour guide during our 2000 trip to Bhutan. Reuniting with Sonam Kesang and Tashi felt surprisingly natural, as if we were long-lost friends. The airport doesn't have a luggage belt, because there are just a couple of flights a day. Instead, there's an area inside the terminal where handlers place the bags, and Sonam Kesang and Tashi quickly gathered our luggage and schlepped it out into Sonam Kesang's dark blue Toyota Land Cruiser.

While securing Claudia's car seat, I noticed a red, white, and blue United States Golf Association bumper sticker on the rear window.

"The USGA told me I'm the only Bhutanese member," said Sonam Kesang.

After months of planning and anticipation, Carrie and I were happy to finally be back in Bhutan. We were also groggy, but we didn't nap during the drive to Thimphu. (Claudia was in a deep sleep the entire way.) It wasn't just that the scenery was so beautiful. I've been to the Rockies, the Alps, and the Adirondacks, and they're all gorgeous habitats. But there's something extra-special about the Himalayas, especially in Bhutan, perhaps because everything is so much bigger. Take the valleys. Bhutan seems like it's a series of nonstop, cavernous, and parallel valleys that zigzag like snakes, and because of this you rarely see snow-capped peaks and can hardly ever see more than a few hundred yards ahead. So as we drove, we were constantly wondering what was around the next bend. Of course, it was always another sun-drenched rice paddy or farm or traditional house made of wood and yak dung. Except for the few cities in Bhutan, the rest of the country is virtually uninhabited, or so it looked to us.

Just a couple of minutes beyond the airport, Carrie burst into laughter.

"Look, it's one of the . . ." she said.

We were in the backseat, and I leaned to the left so my head was over Carrie's lap and I could see out her window. There was a giant penis, light orange, painted on the wall of a house. "The phalluses," I said. "How could we forget?"

The phallus is a Buddhist symbol meant to ward off evil, and many Bhutanese families have them painted on their houses. The Bhutanese never notice the phalluses, but tourists always do, and Carrie and I had taken several pictures of them during our 2000 trip.

More than anything, though, what kept our eyes peeled and our hearts fluttering was the hell-bent and frightening way that Sonam Kesang drove. He whipped around hairpin turns, which occur every 50 yards or so on the sinuous Bhutanese roads that are gouged out of mountainsides, and it felt like he was driving at 100 miles per hour, although it was actually closer to 35.

"When NASCAR has the first Bhutan 500, you'll be the champion," I told Sonam Kesang.

Sonam Kesang smiled. "I like watching NASCAR," he said. "Too bad we don't have races here in Bhutan."

My brow was sweaty. At every turn, I imagined our Land Cruiser rocketing off the edge and tumbling a few hundred feet into a river gorge. Sonam Kesang, on the other hand, looked as placid as if he were tapping in a 3-inch putt. I jokingly asked how often cars fly off the road, figuring that would be a subtle way of asking Sonam Kesang to slow down. I was a guest, and I didn't want to be rude. I also didn't want to be one with the Himalayas, at least not yet.

"It happens," Tashi said. "But not too often."

Sonam Kesang smiled and tapped the accelerator as we roared around another curve.

BEFORE LEAVING NEW YORK, Sonam Kesang had told us that he was going to find a house or apartment for us for our three months in Bhutan. But toward the end of the two-hour drive from Paro to Thimphu, Sonam Kesang said that he hadn't found one. "I looked at a few places," Sonam Kesang said. "But I wasn't sure what you'd like."

"So where are you taking us?" Carrie said.

"To somebody's house," Sonam Kesang replied.

At this point we were driving up the valley, through the center of Thimphu, which was full of lit buildings, stores, and homes. It was pitch black, and Carrie and I were vaguely familiar with the town's layout, but we didn't know it well enough yet to know where we were. After a few minutes, we crossed a little steel bridge above the Thimphu River, and the areas on both sides of the road suddenly looked desolate. We would later learn that we had entered Langjophaka, an upscale and mostly residential section of town. Soon we turned off the main road and onto a very dark and deserted dirt driveway. It felt eerily like nowhere.

"Where are we going?" Carrie said.

"He lives up the road," Sonam Kesang said.

"Who lives up the road?" I asked.

"Uh, well," Sonam Kesang replied, "it's a nice place. . . ."

Sonam Kesang wouldn't tell us the name of our host. Nor did he have a concrete answer as to why, with six months to look, he had been unable to find a place for us. But Sonam Kesang wasn't trying to be rude or evasive. He was simply being Bhutanese. Somehow, though, things always work out in Bhutan.

"This won't work," said Carrie. "I am not staying in some random house in the middle of nowhere with some random man I've never met."

"Should we go home?" I asked.

Carrie wasn't laughing. "I'll take Claudia into town and check into the Druk," Carrie said, referring to what then was the only upscale hotel in Bhutan.

"Good idea," I replied. "We'll get the honeymoon suite and order baked Alaska. After Claudia goes to sleep, we'll relax in the Jacuzzi. It'll be a perfect welcome to the land of gross national happiness."

Carrie still wasn't laughing. Her arms were folded and her lips were pressed tight. "If you think this is funny, you're wrong," she said. "I am not happy."

After twisting back and forth up the bumpy, windy road, Sonam Kesang made a 180-degree turn to the left and slammed on the brakes. "We're here," Sonam Kesang said with a smile.

"Here" was the end of a road on a hillside at the base of a mountain. A mountain to me, but not to the Bhutanese. "This is just a nice hill," said Sonam Kesang.

The land below us was dotted with homes, while above us was dense forest. We were in a dirt driveway 50 feet from a modest two-story house, the highest home on the hillside, and it had a small front porch. It was so dark that I couldn't see what the house looked like, but I did smell cow dung. I looked down on the patchy grass and saw huge piles of the poop. There wasn't any farmland around us, but clearly people weren't the only sentient beings living in the neighborhood.

"This is Dasho Benji's home," Sonam Kesang said.

Sonam Kesang's confident, calm tone made it clear we were supposed to know about Dasho Benji.

As we disembarked from the SUV, I got goose bumps because the scene was so inspiring. I could see every star in the universe. The air was damp, and cicadalike bugs were buzzing. While the dirt road we'd driven up was only one quarter of a mile from the main road, it felt like we were on a mountaintop. Below was a panoramic view of the Thimphu Valley. Only forty years ago the deep valley was lush and undeveloped. There were no paved roads; wild boar and Himalayan black bears were plentiful; and the only buildings of note were monasteries and the massive Thimphu dzong.

Today the dzong and monasteries still stand out, but not as much because a sea of urban sprawl surrounds them. Bhutan doesn't have chain stores or malls—yet—but Thimphu is congested with paved roads, houses, apartment buildings, offices, stores, and electric and phone wires. The nine-hole Royal Thimphu Golf Club is the lone swath of greenery remaining in town.

"Wow!" I said to Carrie. "This is amazing. We're home, in the Himalayas."

"I will not unpack until we've seen the house," Carrie said flatly.

Suddenly three huge cows ambled from behind the house to within a few feet of us. They stopped and began chomping on the grass. I liked the idea that we'd be living among animals.

"Yuck," Carrie said, lifting her right foot to inspect her heel. She had stepped in a pile of poop.

I laughed.

"Ha, ha," Carrie said. "You won't be laughing when you step in it."

"Maybe not," I said. "But Claudia will be laughing when she's playing in the yard and plops into a pile."

Carrie wasn't smiling. "Maybe the gardener will clean it up," she said.

"I think the cows *are* the gardeners," I said.

Sonam Kesang and Tashi carried our bags into the house and said good-bye. "We'll talk tomorrow," Sonam Kesang said.

"How long will we stay here?" I asked.

"No more than a few weeks," Sonam Kesang said. "As soon as we can find a permanent place, you'll move. When I asked around the golf club for a volunteer to house you temporarily, Benji immediately volunteered."

Next, two scraggly bichons frises zoomed out of the front door, which was ajar, and began barking and jumping around as if they expected us to feed them snacks. I was certainly familiar with the breed. My father, who lives in Princeton, New Jersey, has one, as do hordes of New Yorkers. But the breed is definitely not common in Bhutan, where stray mongrels are ubiquitous and the total population of bred dogs could fit in the back of a Land Cruiser. These small, hyperactive canines were the first sign that this was not an ordinary Bhutanese home.

I'LL NEVER FORGET the glasses with the huge lenses, thick black rims, and even thicker arms. Nor will I forget the huge ears, upon which the eyeglass arms rested, with thick lobes jutting out from the sides of that shiny tan scalp. Most memorable, though, were the warmth and grace that Benji expressed. He greeted us as if we were kin as we rumbled across the porch and through the front door, laden with enough luggage to equip a royal caravan.

Benji, whose formal name is Dasho Paljor Jigmie Dorji, stood at the bottom of the staircase wearing khaki pants, a navy blue golf shirt, and a wide smile. As Carrie and I stood there with Claudia, the dogs were barking, jumping, and nipping at my pants.

"Their names?" I asked.

"Bozo and Muffy," said Benji.

I laughed. So did Carrie. Bichons frises named Bozo and Muffy. This was definitely not just another Bhutanese household.

I vaguely remembered Benji. We'd met him briefly at Royal Thimphu when we visited Bhutan as tourists. Now he sported a healthy potbelly, but that seemed like a recent addition, because his nearly 6-foot frame had an athletic, muscular build. He looked like a pint-size retired NFL linebacker.

Benji's reception made me feel like I did back in college when I'd return to Mom's house at the end of a semester. "It's great to have a golf pro in the house," Benji bellowed, his voice firm and raspy. "My game needs help. I hope you fix me up so I can win some money!"

Benji spoke with genuine bonhomie, but also with the authority of a trial lawyer. That was no surprise. Having just turned fifty-nine in August, Benji had recently retired after a storied and variegated career as a civil servant, including a role as the first chief justice of Bhutan. Never mind that he didn't go to law school. In the late 1970s and early 1980s, the king was creating many of the government's divisions from scratch and staffing them with people who didn't have formal training but, like Benji, were smart, devoted to the kingdom, and usually from his family or inner circle of friends. Benji fit both bills, because he's a first cousin to His Majesty. After Benji's stint at the High Court, he served at the Ministry of Social Services and as ambassador to the United Nations in Geneva, and he then helped to create Bhutan's National Environment Commission and the Royal Society for Protection of Nature.

As Carrie, Claudia, and I stood just inside the doorway, Benji walked to the dresser in the foyer. "You guys will love this," he said.

Benji picked up a foot-long green plastic fish from the top of the dresser. The fish was mounted on a piece of wood with a little gold plaque engraved with the following name: *Billy Bass*. Holding the fish in his cupped palms, Benji gently approached Carrie, who was holding Claudia, and held the fish up to Claudia's face. "Press the red button," Benji gently said.

Claudia smiled, but she had no clue what to do. "Okay, I'll press it," Benji said.

After pressing the button, the fish came to life. It began gyrating, its head and tail flapping back and forth, and singing with a thick Jamaican accent. Most of the words were a blur, but I distinctly recall the fish crowing over and over, "Don't worry, be happy." Claudia began laughing. So did Carrie.

Thrilled to have an audience, Benji began dancing in place as he waved the fish up and down in front of Claudia's face. "I paid ten pounds for this beauty in London," Benji said in his clipped British accent. "A damn rip-off! Two weeks after I bought it, I went to New York and saw some guy on the street selling the same damn thing for eight bucks. Oh, well."

A small woman entered the foyer through the door leading to the kitchen. She meekly said with a smile, "Sir, dinner."

"You guys must be starved," Benji said.

"That's an understatement," I said.

"What'll Claudia eat?" Benji asked.

"What are you serving?" I said.

"Kalpana," Benji bellowed. "What's for dinner?"

Kalpana, a Nepalese woman about thirty years old who had been Benji's maid and cook for many years, returned to the foyer from the kitchen. "Sir, spaghetti and broccoli, and spinach soup," she said.

"Great," I said. "Claudia will love it."

Our around-the-world voyage, our sleep deprivation, the encrusted layers of dirt on our bodies—all had been forgotten because Benji's home felt like our home, and we were thoroughly enchanted with having him as our host and entertainer.

We sat around Benji's dining room table, and when I attached the portable plastic baby seat we'd lugged from New York to one of the dining room chairs, Benji laughed. "I love it," he said, looking at Claudia. "That will be your throne."

Kalpana filled the table with bowls of steaming spaghetti, broccoli, tomato sauce with beef, and spinach soup. Everything was homemade and delicious. "I could easily get used to this," Carrie said.

The décor in Benji's house was an attractive and comfortable hodgepodge. The furniture ranged from traditional Bhutanese *chodrums*—low wooden benches with handcarved and hand-painted Buddhist motifs on the sides—to a New England–style dining room table, chairs, and breakfront, which looked like they'd come from Ethan Allen. The walls were adorned with handcarved wooden artifacts, intricate *thangkas*—a type of Buddhist religious painting—and color pictures of famous Bhutanese monuments, including Mount Jhomolhari, the kingdom's most sacred peak and the most popular destination among tourists who trek in Bhutan. Sitting on an armoire in the entryway were two black-and-white pictures that caught my eye: one was a family portrait with twenty people in traditional Bhutanese outfits standing outside in two rows, and the other was a portrait of two dozen buff male students at a military academy dressed in track and field uniforms.

During a trip to the bathroom during dinner, I stopped to look closer at the black-and-white images. Benji came into the foyer. "Guess where I am," Benji said, pointing to the class portrait.

At first, I thought Benji was joking. There can't be a military academy in Bhutan, and even if there is, it can't have those massive Gothic stone buildings like you see at West Point. Still, I didn't want to question my host, so I scanned the picture from left to right. Aha! Benji was easy to locate: Everybody was white except for the Tibetan-looking guy with the huge ears and black glasses.

I pointed to the Tibetan-looking guy.

"You got it," Benji exclaimed. "That's me."

"Where was the picture taken?" I asked.

"Sandhurst," Benji said.

"What's that?" I said.

Benji was puzzled. "You don't know?" he said. "The British Royal Military Academy."

Obviously there was a lot Carrie and I needed to learn about Benji.

"It's the British West Point," Benji said. "I was commissioned in the summer of 1966. What a *fantastic* institution!"

Whoa! Here we were in the middle of the Himalayas with a man who had imported bichons frises, had been the Bhutanese John Jay, enjoyed gambling on the golf course and traveling to England to attend horse races, and had attended the vaunted Sandhurst Academy, the same place that had graduated Sir Winston Churchill. This was definitely not the typical Bhutanese citizen described by our flowery guidebooks.

I then turned my attention to the family snapshot. "Is this your family?" I asked.

Benji smiled and pointed his right index finger at a young man with penetrating black eyes. "Yes," Benji said. "And that is the king."

Now I felt silly. Benji continued, pointing to an elegant and elderly lady in a flowing *kira*, the traditional ground-length garment worn by women in Bhutan. A kira is a woven and rectangular-shaped piece of fabric that is wrapped around the body and worn over a blouse. "That is the queen mother," he told us.

BENJI'S FAMILY IS one of the most influential in the history of Bhutan, and they're descendants of Tibetan and Sikkimese bloodlines. Wedged between Nepal (to the west) and Bhutan (to the east), the Himalayan territory known as Sikkim is one of the twenty-two states that comprise India, and it's by far the smallest state, with only 2,740 square miles, making it less than half the size of Connecticut.

In Bhutan, the Dorjis rose to prominence when the monarchy was created at the beginning of the twentieth century. The first king appointed Benji's great-grandfather Kazi Ugyen Dorji as the Bhutan agent—akin to the U.S. secretary of state and essentially the liaison with the outside world—and stationed him in Kalimpong, India, because the bulk of Bhutan's external activities involved the British in India and the Indians themselves. Benji's grandfather Raja Sonam Tobgay Dorji was the second Bhutan agent, and then Benji's father, Jigme Palden Dorji, became the third. In 1958, the king was so pleased with Jigme Palden's work that he promoted him to be the country's first prime minister.

Still today, Jigme Palden is the most famous Dorji, mainly because he is a true pioneer of modern Bhutan. Although the third king gets most of the credit, even in history textbooks, for spearheading Bhutan's decision to end its isolation and start down the road toward modernization, it was Jigme Palden who did much of the groundwork. He initiated the creation of basic infrastructure, including schools, hospitals, roads, and electricity, and began the long process of rooting out rampant government corruption and cronyism. With regard to the latter, Jigme Palden was taking a big risk. Those in comfortable positions didn't want their status to change, and some were insecure about the country's changing identity and the possibility of losing unmerited perks such as cars with drivers and tuition payments for their children to attend foreign schools.

On April 15, 1964, Jigme Palden was murdered in Phuentsholing, a town in southern Bhutan on the Indian border, on his way back from Calcutta. He was shot while eating dinner in a bungalow with one of his brothers and some friends. His final words, uttered while bleeding to death in the arms of his wife, a Tibetan woman named Tessla, were, "My king, my king, tell my king that I served him as best I could," and then "*Sangeyla chyapsum cheo*," a prayer whose translation is "I take refuge in the Buddha."

The murder is the country's greatest unsolved mystery, with all the intrigue of JFK's assasination. Nobody debates that the gun used to kill Jigme Palden was a gift from the third king to his Tibetan mistress and that the bullets were fired by Bhutanese Army soldiers, but there is no clear picture of who masterminded the assassination.

Benji and his two brothers always seemed uncomfortable discussing the details of the assassination with me, which was understandable. Instead, they suggested that I read *Bhutan: The Dragon Kingdom in Crisis*, by Nari Rustomji. Rustomji was an Indian diplomat who was brought to Bhutan in the mid-1950s to work as the right-hand man and top adviser to Jigme Palden and the third king. After completing his assignment in Bhutan in the early 1970s, Rustomji embarked on a writing career, and *Bhutan: The Dragon Kingdom* is one of his best works, a superbly detailed book that is the only critical examination of Jigme Palden's assassination and the Dorji family's history. My problem was finding a copy of the book. It seemed like there was a conspiracy to keep all copies out of the country.

When I finally laid hands on the book, I discovered a host of fascinating possible plotlines for assassination. Early in 1963, the third king had a heart attack and was forced to spend most of the rest of his life abroad getting medical care, and in his absence the king asked Jigme Palden to assume administration of the kingdom. It's no secret that Jigme Palden infuriated high-ranking monks and army officers by greatly reducing their powers and in many cases taking away their jobs. So did senior army officers kill Jigme Palden out of jealousy? Or perhaps the army officers killed Jigme Palden out of devotion to the king, with the intention of returning the country's ruling authority back to the king.

After an investigation, Chabda Namgyal, the king's uncle and the commander in chief of the army at the time of Jigme Palden's death, was reportedly held responsible for the assassination. To be sure, Namgyal had a key role in the assassination, and it is likely that Namgyal had ordered one of his corporals, Jambey, to fire the bullets that killed Jigme Palden. Nonetheless, Namgyal was convicted, sentenced to death, and executed. (In 2004 the king issued a royal decree that abolished capital punishment in Bhutan.)

Namgyal's death, however, was not the end of the saga, because few Bhutanese believe that he was solely responsible for the assassination plot. More likely, Namgyal was under orders from a higher authority when he directed the corporal to kill Jigme Palden. It's possible, for example, that the king himself ordered Namgyal to murder Jigme Palden. Why? Because the king was rumored to have been jealous of the prominence that the Dorji family was gaining in Bhutan, even though the king had helped foster the Dorjis' high stature. An even more spectacular theory involves allegations against the third king's longtime Tibetan mistress. According to Rustomji, the mistress might have been a spy for the Tibetan government working as part of a plot to take over Bhutan, or she might have been masterminding the plot herself.

The mystery of Jigme Palden's assassination might never be solved. One thing, however, is certain: His legacy lives on in

Bhutan. Jigme Palden's three sons—Benji, Tobgye, and Kalden—all followed in their father's footsteps by devoting themselves to Bhutan with distinguished careers as civil servants and businessmen.

BACK AT THE dinner table at Benji's, as we feasted on a freshly baked apple pie, Benji stood and looked at his watch. It was eight-thirty P.M. "Excuse me, I've got to go upstairs and change," he said. "I have a date tonight."

On his way out, Benji stopped. "Do you want to come along?" he asked.

Carrie and I both looked at Claudia, whose blissfully red cheeks were covered with apple pie. We then in sync turned our gazes back up to Benji.

"Don't worry about my dear Claudia," Benji said. "Kalpana will take care of her. We're going to dance and play snooker in town. You'll have a great time."

"Thanks, Benji," I said. "But I think we'll lay low tonight."

Carrie, the family's social butterfly and nocturnal adventurer, had another idea. "I'll come," she said.

After Carrie and Benji left, I went upstairs with Claudia. Our bedroom, one of three on the second floor of Benji's house, be-longed to Benji's nineteen-year-old daughter, Sonam Choden, who was a freshman at the University of New Brunswick in Canada. Her bedroom looked like the bedroom of any Ameri-can collegian. There was a boom box on her wooden dresser, and next to the dresser was an armoire full of blue jeans, fancy shirts, dresses, and shoes. (Carrie was most interested in the shoe collection, which included several pairs of black high heels.) A *Pearl Harbor* movie poster hung on a wall, and on Sonam's desk were several photo albums full of the same type of pictures that Carrie has in her school-day albums—bubbly teenage girls hugging each other and beaming megawatt smiles.

By ten-thirty P.M., Claudia was fast asleep while clutching her stuffed Winnie the Pooh with her right arm. She was in the blue portable crib we'd lugged from New York. I sat on the porch outside our bedroom, my eyes focused on the Thimphu dzong, which was illuminated by floodlights and just half a mile away. The panorma of the monstrous dzong was mesmerizing. It felt like I'd been transported into a King Arthur storybook.

My eyes wandered up the valley walls to the black sky teeming with stars. I wondered who and what were in the vastness. Perhaps way up above and beyond the valley walls there were yak herders sleeping? Maybe a snow leopard hunting? Legend has it that the yeti, aka Sasquatch, lives in the Bhutanese Himalayas, and at this moment not even the presence of the yeti seemed too preposterous to believe.

We had come so far, to another world, another universe. But part of me also felt happily close to home.

Chapter 3

LORD BUDDHA, MEET
LORD LONG BALL

THE THIRD TEE at Royal Thimphu is in the middle of the course, and just behind the tee is an unusual hazard: a large Buddhist shrine, called a chorten. Chortens are ubiquitous in Bhutan and come in various shapes and sizes, ranging from small huts the size of a subway token booth to enormous domes adorned with tall golden spires. Royal Thimphu's chorten is modest, with walls that are 25 feet long and 20 feet tall. Like most others, it has walls of rocks held together by yak dung, and the roof consists of wooden beams covered with little slabs of slate. Its walls are nondescript; they're painted white and encircled near the top by a 2-foot-tall blood-red band, an identifying symbol for all religious buildings in Bhutan. For many decades this chorten was a center for religious devotion; for the past twenty years it's been a holy target for golfers dreaming of John Daly–like drives.

Royal Thimphu is one of seven courses in the kingdom but the only one with a bona fide layout, and it's the only one open to the public. Any Bhutanese who has the will and the means to pay the $180 annual membership fee and the daily greens fee

($2.25 on weekdays, $3.35 on weekends) can play. Foreigners are welcome, too; expatriate residents pay a $500 annual fee (greens fee rates are the same as for the Bhutanese), and daily guests pay $50 for eighteen holes. Five of the other courses are on military bases and one is at India House, the Indian embassy compound in Thimphu.

The topography at Royal Thimphu is similar to that at a British links, except the ground is hillier. But the course isn't a series of Himalayan ups and downs. With a couple of exceptions, the terrain rolls gently and has generous fairways. The course sits on a wide-open, 48-acre, amoeba-shaped parcel that is comprised of fairways, greens, tees, some small greenside bunkers, thick roughs, and just a few very small pine trees scattered about. The clubhouse steps have a wonderfully dramatic view. From there, you have a 180-degree panoramic look at the Thimphu Valley in the distance, while up close you can see every hole on the course, the chorten, and the hugely imposing Thimphu dzong, which sits across the property and adjacent to the fifth fairway. The clubhouse sits on the northern edge of the course and along a road that is just above the eighth and ninth holes and is separated from the holes by bushes and a chain-link fence. This northern edge of the property rises gradually from the clubhouse for about 800 yards until it reaches the high point of the course, the eighth tee. That tee is about 150 feet higher than the course's lowest point, the fifth fairway.

The 2,700-yard course doesn't look especially difficult. The bunkers are few in number and small and shallow in shape; the lone exception is the deep trap that's well below and 15 yards in front of the second green. Also, there aren't many water hazards: just the small creek crossing the fifth fairway, a pond in front of the seventh tee (in play for only a dribbler or pop-up), and greenside ponds at the first, second, and seventh holes. And every hole is relatively straight except for the fifth, a 90-degree dogleg left. But scoring is tough at Royal Thimphu. The greens are tiny, averaging 1,500 square feet, and most of them are surrounded by swales that catch even mildly wayward approaches. Then there's the course's most punishing hazard: the rough. A mélange of thick fescue and other dense shrubs, the rough grows unabated during the spring, summer, and fall, often reaching above your waist, because the monsoons are so strong and the club doesn't have mowers big or strong enough to cut such flora. Also, there is just one narrow intermediate cut of rough, so that makes pretty much every drive an all-or-nothing proposition.

Before the golf course was built, the chorten was one of Thimphu's most revered holy spots. Bhutanese visitors to the chorten were required to stop and pray; monks and laypeople used to meditate there; and women occasionally delivered babies in it. After the golf course opened, however, the chorten fell into disuse, but it wasn't razed. According to Buddhist tradition, chortens are built on sites deemed propitious by monks, and a chorten can't be destroyed unless a senior monk says it no longer has good karma. That's why chortens are sometimes in bizarre places. For example, there's a chorten in the middle of one of Thimphu's busiest roads—a road we drove on every day because it's between Benji's house and the center of town—and the road sweeps around the chorten in both directions.

Over the past few decades, as golf has attracted a small following, however, the chorten at Royal Thimphu has been regaining its devotional importance. Royal Thimphu's members worship at the chorten perhaps more fervently than people used to. The golfers dream about it. They lustily stare at it. They pray for the day that they'll be able to reach its sacred walls. But it's not Lord

Buddha whom the Bhutanese golfers think about when they look at the chorten. It's Lord Long Ball.

Bhutanese golfers, like hackers everywhere, crave distance. So every day the men at practice would hardly try to improve their technique; they'd do what golfers do at driving ranges around the world. They'd launch drive after drive, hoping to hit one shot longer than the next. In this case, their target was the chorten, 500 yards from the tee. (The second and third holes are parallel.) It didn't matter that nobody had a chance of reaching the chorten, thin air, souped-up equipment, and my expert instruction be damned.

"I NEED HELP," said Yougs.

"That's why I'm here," I said.

"I'd love to win the Bhutan Open," Yougs said. "With your help, I might be able to do that."

I didn't know what to say. Teaching golf had seemed easy enough back at home, when I used to give casual tips to friends and Carrie. But now I was being paid to impart sage advice that was supposed to make people play better. I'd been playing golf for thirty years, but it was always as an impassioned amateur. Now, technically, I was a professional. I must have been: My lesson rate, according to a notice on the bulletin board in the clubhouse, was 150 ngultrums (about $4) per hour. Still, I didn't feel much like a golf pro.

And there was an added bit of pressure. The day before, Palden Tshering had driven me home after playing nine relaxed holes. Palden, who would be a frequent playing partner in Bhutan, was about thirty, the father of two little girls, and a diehard golfer who used his size (6'1" and 190 pounds) to hammer monstrous drives. His father is a career diplomat, having served as Bhutan's ambassador to the United Nations in New York and as diplomat to Bangladesh, India, Japan, and Nepal. Palden's father-in-law, Dasho Lhendup Dorji, is a businessman, one of the richest men in the country, and a brother of the late prime minister Jigme Palden Dorji.

Palden lives on the outskirts of Thimphu at a sprawling estate with apple orchards and gardens that include the only artichoke patch in the kingdom. As a boy, though, he spent several years in America in Scarsdale, a suburb 25 miles north of New York City, while his father was the ambassador to the United Nations. It was fun to hear Palden regale me with a Bhutanese perspective on living in America during the go-go 1980s. "Wild place," Palden said. "Loved it, but holy cow. Everybody was always running like crazy, even when they were just going to the store. I never understood the big rush."

Palden never felt completely at home in Scarsdale. He says few Americans truly understood his heritage and that many people naïvely assumed his life in Bhutan was like an outtake from *Wild Kingdom*. "I was shocked at how many people asked me, 'Are there bathrooms in Bhutan?'" said Palden. "One person even asked, 'Do you use toilet paper over there?'"

"Were you sad when you had to go back to Bhutan?" I asked.

"Just a little," Palden replied. "I liked it over there, and it was a bummer to leave my friends. But this is home."

Next, Palden asked me a question. "Hey, man, I've been dying to ask you something," said Palden. "Are you *really* Tiger's coach?"

My eyeballs nearly popped out of their sockets. "Me? Tiger's teacher?" Like Tiger Woods, he meant? "Uhhh, not in this lifetime."

Palden seemed genuinely surprised. "Really?" he said. "You've *never* taught Tiger?"

"Sorry," I said. "I'm just a golf writer. This is my first real teaching gig."

Where on earth was this coming from? Did I know Tiger Woods? Didn't most American hackers hit flop shots and eat cheeseburgers with Phil Mickelson? Did they have bathrooms in Bhutan? I fiddled with the latch on the glove compartment and racked my brain.

Oh—the book. A few months before leaving New York, I sent Sonam Kesang a copy of the instructional book *In Every Kid There Lurks a Tiger*, which I wrote with Rudy Duran, who was Tiger's first instructor and who worked with him from ages four to ten. Then I forgot all about it. My new students, apparently, had not.

"The guys at the club have been salivating," Palden said. "Sonam Kesang told people about that book, and I guess everybody just kind of assumed. They've been thinking they're going to get tips from Tiger's man."

"We'd better keep this little bit of news just between us," Palden continued. "If guys find out that you're not Tiger's coach, they'll be majorly bummed."

I was worried. Would people be mad if they learned that I'd never taught Tiger? Should I tell people the real story and kill the rumor? Would the club send me home if they found out? I decided to remain silent unless somebody raised the subject.

I anxiously changed the topic to the first thing at hand: Palden's car. He was driving a tiny four-door Maruti hatchback that was smaller than a VW Beetle, a peculiar choice for somebody whose father-in-law was one of the kingdom's richest men. "Why are you driving this little matchbox?" I said.

Palden leaned over to me with a huge grin. "This is my trophy," he said. "I won it in the India House tournament a couple
of years ago."

"Did you make a hole in one or something?" I said, wondering how he'd won a car in an amateur golf tournament.

Palden explained that first prize is always a car at the annual
India House tournament. "That's why every golfer in the country comes to play," Palden said.

"What about the rules of amateur status?" I said. According to
The Rules of Golf, you lose your amateur status and become a
professional for accepting a prize worth more than $750, and
a new Maruti costs at least $3,000.

Palden shrugged his shoulders. "This is Bhutan, man," he said.
"I guess we're all pros, because nobody ever follows that rule."

Surely in this nation of pros, I could be a pro, too, right? I just
didn't quite feel like a Tiger yet.

So it was a blessing that Ugyen "Yougs" Dorji (no relation to
Benji) was my first pupil. On a sunny Tuesday morning at ten,
Yougs and I were alone on the practice tee. I hadn't been scheduled to begin teaching for a couple of days and had come to play
a few holes, but while I was walking toward the first green,
which was by the practice tee, Yougs asked if I'd help him.

Yougs was one of the mellowest people I met in a country
that epitomizes mellowness. A thirty-two-year-old tour company and nightclub owner, he was a golfing maniac who spent
part of almost every day at the course playing and practicing. He
had three children (two daughters and one son, between three
and six years old), but they passed their days either in school or
with their nanny, while his wife, who has a degree from Yale's
Graduate School of Forestry and Environmental Studies, worked
in the sustainable development division at the Ministry of Finance.

Yougs was thrilled when his wife got accepted to Yale, but not because it's one of the greatest schools in the world.

"What a golf course!" he said, referring to the world-famous Yale University layout designed by Charles Blair MacDonald.

"Did you play there a lot?" I asked.

Yougs's smile turned to a frown. "Never. Too damn expensive," he said.

"Did you play anywhere?" I inquired.

"No. It was awful. I was dying to play but couldn't afford to," he said.

I started my first official lesson by having Yougs hit 50-yard wedges to the practice-tee landing area, which comprises part of the fairway on the second hole and a huge swath of thick rough to the left of the ninth hole. I talked to Yougs about lag—the angle between the club shaft and the left arm and wrist (for right-handers)—and the need to sustain as much lag as possible until just before impact.

To prepare to teach in Bhutan, I solicited advice from two teachers who are friends. One was Ben Doyle, an instructor at the Quail Lodge in Carmel, California. Doyle is best known for his close affiliation with *The Golfing Machine*, a seminal instructional tome, and for the dozens of tour players he's worked with. So I flew to California to spend a few days shadowing Doyle on the lesson tee and talking about teaching technique. Doyle loves teaching gadgets, and I left California with a bevy of his favorites to bring to Bhutan. They included a personalized teaching mat, a plastic tarp the size of a king mattress, and some Frisbee-shaped rubber cushions you stand on to stay balanced.

I also got help from Rudy Duran, another Californian from the sleepy coastal town of San Luis Obispo. Duran's advice was much less technical than Doyle's. Duran shared three key concepts:

make sure students have fun on the lesson tee; teach them to play games at practice (see how high they can hit a driver) and at play (try to hit balls into a garbage can while waiting to tee off); and encourage everbody to hit the ball as hard as possible. "To swing easy is to swing like a dummy," Duran said. "You've got to whap the ball."

I shared Duran's three keys with Yougs, and he liked them. I then told Yougs that the funky way he picks up the club in his backswing, rather than letting it flow smoothly back and up on a gentle arc, was okay. "Tour players have lots of wacky moves in their swings, but they all produce a ton of lag and hold it until the moment of truth," I said.

"Even Jim Furyk?" Yougs asked.

I excused myself and hustled up to the clubhouse to get from my backpack some golf magazines with swing sequences of several tour players, including Furyk. Yougs was surprised that every pro had lots of lag.

"I guess I need to learn that," he said.

I then returned to the clubhouse to get an impact bag, one of the golf training aids I'd brought from the States. An impact bag is a bright yellow bag the size of a huge watermelon made of thick plastic. You stuff the bag full of towels, and you use it by trying to propel the bag forward by hitting the clubhead against it. If you create and sustain lag through impact, you move the bag forward so it slides along the turf.

The first few swings that Yougs took didn't move the bag. I then took a couple of swings in slow motion to demonstrate the technique, and each time I made sure my wrists remained cocked and the clubhead remained well behind my hands as I hit the bag with it. Doing that propelled the bag forward. Yougs then copied me and moved the bag, too.

"Good deal," he said. "I like it."

Next I showed Yougs an address routine that Doyle had taught me and which is used in some form by many tour professionals. You start by placing your right foot down about six inches away from the ball and perpendicular to the target line while your left foot is behind your back on the ground and parallel to the right foot or even slightly farther back from the target. Standing like that creates a little tension in your lower back. Then you look back and forth a couple of times from the ball to the target to be sure you're properly aligned. Next you slide your left foot forward and onto the target line so it's in position to hit, then you slide your right foot away from your left foot and into position and then you're ready to swing away.

As Yougs practiced the new address routine, he was as focused as an archer staring down a target, and he was sweating profusely. He was so meticulous that he sometimes went through the routine a half dozen times before he felt he'd done it well enough and was properly aligned to swing away and hit a shot.

While practicing Yougs took breaks every minute or so to puff on a cigarette dangling from his mouth. He even left the cigarette in his mouth while hitting. That reminded me of a picture of Ben Hogan, a big smoker, in midswing with a cigarette dangling from his mouth and a big cylinder of ash still attached to the cigarette.

"I don't want to advocate smoking," I said, "but you might try to get a chunk of ash on a cigarette and then swing with the cigarette in your mouth. You can learn to stay in perfect balance by swinging while trying to not let the ash fall off the cigarette."

After forty-five minutes, I left Yougs to practice on his own. It was nearly eleven and nobody else was around, so I went up to the clubhouse to have an early lunch. I had white rice and double-fried pork, which were delicious and became my quotidian midday meal. I also had a slice of freshly baked pound cake for dessert. Then some golfers began arriving to hit practice balls during their lunch breaks.

I went down to the practice tee and stood in the background watching the three or four guys swing. One of them, Kinga, asked me to analyze his swing, which I gladly did. I spread out a 4-foot-by-6-foot plastic mat with words and anatomical drawings that explain the golf swing and had Kinga stand on it. I walked him through the grip, stance, and address routine. Then I had him swing into the impact bag, and I used the video camera I'd bought back in New York just for teaching golf on this trip. I was amazed when I looked at video of Kinga. He had real lag while hitting balls with his wedge. He was attacking the ball with vigor, his club pouncing down and into it, and he was in perfect balance.

A steady trickle of golfers appeared on the tee throughout the afternoon, and I spent a little time with each of them. By the end of the day my fear had vanished and I was perfectly confident that the advice I was sharing wasn't hot air. The proof was that the men were smiling and thanking me, and even more, their balls were flying on crisp, straight arcs.

A COUPLE OF days later, at about three P.M., ten guys were on the lesson tee chatting and hitting balls. I'd already been at the course since eight-thirty A.M. and given several lessons. The golfers kept coming for help, and I was eager to give it. My only break was for lunch. By now I'd been teaching for a few days and I felt like a golf pro. People were calling me at home and the course to schedule lessons and, best of all, they were paying me ngultrums. The fact that people were paying me for golf instruction was thrilling.

"Coach!" Benji yelled. "Come over here! I think I've got it!"

Benji had watched me show the address routine I'd first shown to Yougs to several more people, and now Benji, too, was trying to do it. I walked over to the other side of the practice tee where Benji was hitting balls.

"Looks good," I said. "You're a quick study."

"Don't help him," said Yougs. "He's hopeless."

Sonam Kesang was also on the practice tee, hitting drivers with his long and fluid swing. "I had some lessons in Bangkok," Sonam Kesang said. "Huge help."

Amid the golf banter and ball beating, I was more focused on the dzong. I heard rhythmic chanting and drumbeats reverberating from it. "What's going on?" I asked Sonam Kesang.

"The performers are practicing," he replied. "The *tsechu* starts tomorrow."

A tsechu is a religious festival. Virtually every region in Bhutan has at least one tsechu a year, and they're held in the main courtyard of the local dzong or palace. Lasting up to three days, the tsechus are centered around monks who dance and play instruments while acting out religious and cultural folktales. Bhutanese of all ages flock to the tsechus, sometimes walking for a day or more and staying in town with family or friends, and spend all day watching the performances and enjoying the festive atmosphere around the dzong or palace. Outside of the performance area, vendors hawk trinkets, clothing, and food, and there are booths in which you can play games for fun (tossing a ball into a basket, for example) or gamble by playing card games.

I asked Sonam Kesang when he'd go to the Thimphu tsechu so that I could make plans to accompany him.

"Nah," Sonam Kesang replied. "I'm not going."

"Why not?" I asked.

"The tsechu isn't such a big deal anymore," said Sonam Kesang. "As a kid, I used get all excited. It was a very big deal. I'd wear my best gho, Mom would pack lunch, give me 20 ngultrums, and at six-thirty in the morning my friends and I would run down to the dzong here in Thimphu. Now, though, lots of people skip the tsechu. We have too many diversions—things like golf, TV, and computers—so we're losing touch with the traditional ways."

Sonam Kesang was still hitting balls while talking. "I'm also not looking for dates anymore," he continued. "The tsechus are a big pickup scene for the kids. People go to be seen and to meet somebody special."

Another urgent call from Benji interrupted the conversation.

"Coach, Coach, this is wonderful," Benji said while hitting little wedges. His golf shirt was soaked from perspiration, and beads of sweat on top of his shiny bald scalp were glimmering in the sunlight. He was creating and sustaining lag, remaining balanced, and pounding down into the ball, cleanly nipping the shots and sending the balls on crisp little arcs out into the range.

I gazed across the Thimphu River to Langjophaka, where I could see Benji's yellow house on the hillside. Perhaps Claudia and Carrie were there playing in the yard? Maybe Carrie had left and was on her way to the course for our date to play a few holes together later this afternoon? A couple of days ago, Kalpana had offered to babysit for Claudia until we got a full-time nanny for when Carrie began her job with the chief justice in a couple of weeks, and we liked Kalpana so much that we hired her as our temporary babysitter.

It had been just a couple of weeks since we had left New York, but I was already beginning to feel like I might be able to make a career as a golf pro. Was I being naïve? Was it just beginner's luck? Was my head buried in the sand?

All I knew for sure was this: I genuinely enjoyed working on the practice tee. I enjoyed standing behind people and holding my hands on their waists to maintain their balance and having them hit twenty 1-foot putts in a row to ingrain in them what it feels, sounds, and looks like when you make a putt. I enjoyed watching my pupils progress, often in a single hour-long lesson, from duffing the ball to hitting solid shots. They didn't always hit it well, of course, but a few pure shots in a lesson is enough to satisfy a pupil. Hitting it well consistently just requires more practice.

"Coach, you've fixed all of us, so now why don't you show us what you've got?" said Sonam Kesang.

It was late afternoon, on a Friday, and my confidence had been soaring. But it wasn't from playing well myself. Indeed, I hadn't played a single hole since arriving. Golf teachers always complain that they rarely have the time or the energy to play, and I'd certainly learned that peculiar truth during my first week in Bhutan.

Sonam Kesang handed me his 7-iron, and I was suddenly nervous. A few other golfers were practicing, but they stopped to watch. I felt like the little kid in class whom the teacher calls on and the other children go silent waiting for the kid to reply. I took a couple of practice swings and rolled a few of Sonam Kesang's practice balls over to my feet. Even the caddies who were standing out in the second fairway to shag balls were staring at me, wondering how I'd perform.

I took a deep breath. I rolled a ball onto a tuft of grass with the club and addressed it. I focused my eye on the inside quadrant of the ball and thought about trying to hit down at it, as Ben Doyle told me to do. Somehow I made a great swing and nipped the ball perfectly.

"Nice shot," Sonam Kesang said. "You must be a pro."

Chapter 4

HUNTING FOR RAZORS
IN THIMPHU

STANDING IN THE small bathroom on the second floor of Benji's house, I stared at my reflection in the mirror above the sink and fearfully wondered, How will I survive? Carrie and I were going to a dinner party with the senior editors at *Kuensel* in a few hours, and I had a scraggly beard but couldn't shave because my electric razor didn't work. I'd plugged it in using an electric adapter and the two circular heads spun, but barely. The problem was that I didn't know how to shave with a manual razor. I'd tried using a manual razor once, as a thirteen-year-old summer camper in Maine, but I sliced my lip that day and had never touched a manual razor again.

Ideas whirred as I gazed in the mirror. Maybe I could grow a beard and not shave for three months? No. Maybe I could find an electric razor in Thimphu? Unlikely. Perhaps I could go to a barbershop in Thimphu every couple of days to get a shave? Impractical. So now I faced my first real quandary in Bhutan. It wasn't life or death, to be sure, but I was nervous.

Carrie wasn't home. Neither was Benji. So I called Tashi Wangchuk, who'd been our tour guide in 2000. Since we'd arrived in Bhutan a couple of weeks ago, Tashi had been a good friend, chauffeuring us around Thimphu, introducing us to friends, and even doing some babysitting.

Thankfully, Tashi was home, at his tiny studio apartment in a concrete building in the heart of Thimphu. Tashi worked as a freelance tour guide and was in Thimphu waiting for his next assignment. Twenty minutes later, he drove up to Benji's house in a dated gray Toyota Corolla with black leather seats and parked on the dirt driveway. When I greeted Tashi at the front door, I invited him to come inside while I finished getting my backpack together.

Tashi hesitated. "I'll wait outside," he said.

"No, come inside. We can have some cookies," I said.

"No, thanks," Tashi said. "Dasho might be home, so you just come out when you're ready."

I didn't yet know all the rules of Bhutan's strict unwritten code of social etiquette, but I knew enough to sense what was happening. It would have been inappropriate for Tashi to enter Benji's house without Benji's invitation. Benji, because of his royal bloodlines and professional accomplishments, was much higher on the social ladder than Tashi, who nonetheless was from a fairly prominent Bhutanese family.

A few minutes later I came outside, got into the Corolla, and we left for downtown Thimphu, a mile and a half away.

Tashi, a twenty-seven-year-old bachelor, has long aspired to become Bhutan's first novelist, but that won't be easy. Bhutan has no book publishing companies, and even if there were publishers, the market is small. The adult literacy rate is just 47 percent, with perhaps as many as two hundred thousand people in rural areas who can't read a word. Also, Tashi, whose favorite author is Jack Kerouac, has writer's block. "I've started dozens of stories, but I can only seem to do a few pages and then my mind freezes. So all my stories have only beginnings," said Tashi.

To support himself, Tashi used his advanced English and love of the outdoors to become a tour guide. Typical guides earn a piddling salary of no more than $20 a day, but gratuities for a group of five on a ten-day tour can be as high as $500. So even though the tourist seasons are short in Bhutan—a couple of months in the fall and a couple more in the spring—Tashi needs to handle only a handful of groups during each season to earn several thousand dollars a year. That would be peanuts in New York, but it's a lot of money in Bhutan and enough to support yourself. Even in Thimphu, by far Bhutan's most expensive city, a Bhutanese can rent a modest studio apartment for $200 a month (real estate prices are exorbitantly hiked up for foreigners, who pay up to $700 a month for two-bedroom apartments).

As we drove, I said, "Is there a barbershop we can go to? I need a shave."

"We'll try, but I think they're all closed," Tashi replied.

That sounded preposterous. "Closed?" I said. "It's three in the afternoon."

Tashi didn't reply. He clearly knew something about the barbers that I didn't.

Instead of politely asking Tashi why the barbers were closed, I brusquely said, "Let's go. Maybe we'll get lucky."

I love Thimphu's atmosphere. It mixes the vibrant energy of a big city with Buddhist culture and the tranquillity of the Himalayas. People are everywhere, and they walk in a million directions on sidewalks and in the streets, but you never feel harried because the Bhutanese move slowly and casually. They also smile. Not always, but a lot more than New Yorkers.

I do not love Thimphu, however, for its looks. It's definitely not pretty. Yes, the surrounding mountains are drop-dead stunning and the gorging Thimphu River and Royal Thimphu are beautiful. But the city, wedged in the bottom of a narrow valley, is, like most Asian capitals, overcrowded, overdeveloped, and noisy. It's a pint-size concrete jungle, if you will.

The tangled web of streets that whip and wind in a million directions reminds me of Paris and Rome, as do the narrow roads that are choked with cars, taxis, motor scooters, little trucks, dogs, and buses. Bicycles? None. Ditto for town planning. That's because until recently there were no zoning laws, leaving people to build whatever they wanted wherever they wanted. So it's common to see bizarre juxtapositions, like one block with four- to six-floor concrete commercial buildings sitting next to a block with little wooden homes next to a block with a hospital.

The lack of zoning regulations led to several things being built that should never have been constructed. A few years ago, somebody who owned a mini-mall in the heart of Thimphu wanted to make some extra money, so she decided to sell the parking lot for the mall. Never mind that the buyer planned to raze the parking lot and build another mall on the land, which would leave no parking for either mall and cause massive traffic snarls. The deal went through, and traffic has been much worse ever since.

Thimphu's residents also are an eclectic mix. There are elderly folk in ghos and kiras with weather-beaten skin who look like they've spent the past four decades toiling on farms, and there are young women in elegant silk kiras with Chanel sunglasses and Louis Vuitton handbags.

Perhaps the most ubiquitous creatures are stray dogs. There are well over five thousand of them, and many are out for blood. Indeed, an average of three people a day go to the hospital in Thimphu to be treated for stray-dog bites. The howling canines would likely have been eradicated by now if not for Bhutan's deep Buddhist mores. Several campaigns to kill the strays have had strong support from the government and private citizens, including one program in the 1970s that offered five ngultrums for each dead dog brought to veterinary officials. But Buddhists aren't supposed to kill sentient beings, and each kill-the-dogs campaign has been quashed before it had time to have much effect.

Thimphu's commercial district is centered around a main two-lane road that's a mile long and is set on a hillside that's across the Thimphu River from Benji's house. The road is lined with a hodgepodge of buildings. Some are one- and two-floor decrepit wooden structures decorated in the traditional Bhutanese architectural style: the façades are covered with colorful Buddhist symbols, and the windows are rectangular with a trefoil-like top. Other buildings are new concrete complexes that rise up to as many as four floors, and they, too, have the trefoil windows.

All of the structures have one thing in common: They're jam-packed with shoebox-size shops that are themselves jam-packed with stuff that is virtually all imported because Bhutan has no industrial capability. Several tertiary roads jut out in all directions from the main road, either heading up the hill toward the Moithitang section of town or down the hill toward the Changlimithang soccer stadium and the river.

In Thimphu more than anywhere else in the country, it is clear that Bhutan stands at a real crossroads in its history. You can see the juxtaposition of old and new everywhere. In the 1970s the population was well below ten thousand, and the city looked more like a mountainous outpost than a capital city. Indeed, Thimphu was mostly forest with just a smattering of roads, stores, and houses. Benji and his brother Tobgye used to see wild boar roam around their homes. "Thimphu wasn't jungle land," said Tobgye. "But it was close."

Things have dramatically changed. Now the population has swelled tenfold, the only undeveloped green space is the golf course, and construction crews toil everywhere. In the center of town, offices, stores, and apartment complexes are going up in every nook and cranny. In more residential areas, people are sub-dividing and selling their yards, just like in America. To take advantage of well-heeled guests who pay the $200-per-day tariff that includes lodging, meals, transportation, and guides, luxury hotels have begun popping up, most notably the Aman properties, which cost up to $1,000 a night above the standard daily tariff.

The real estate boom has caused skyrocketing prices. One expert who owns a residential apartment building in Thimphu offered an assessment of the real estate market. "For agricultural land, the value has doubled in the last ten years everyplace," she said. "And it has increased up to five times in sought-after places like the Bumthang Valley." (Bumthang is a district in central Bhutan.)

Urban areas have seen even bigger jumps. "Value has increased ten times in twenty years in township areas, and in Thimphu and Phuentsholing [a city in southern Bhutan on the Indian border and a thriving commercial hub] the increases could be even higher," she continued. The expert then gave an example from her experience. "I looked at land in Thimphu in 1983 and then you could buy one good acre with a good view for twenty-five thousand dollars. Now it would be difficult to find a half acre for five hundred thousand dollars."

In town, boys wear fake Nike sneakers and World Wrestling

Entertainment T-shirts underneath their ghos. There is no Mc-Donald's, but pizza shops have begun sprouting up; if you're ever in town, I highly recommend the yak pies at Seasons, a pizza and pasta joint in the Hong Kong Market section of Thimphu just above the main road. Carrie and I spent many nights at Seasons after Peter Hansen, a Norwegian consultant at the Ministry of Agriculture, told us about it. He raved about it one day while Carrie and I had joined him at Royal Thimphu and were whizzing around with him during one of the forty-five-minute, nine-hole rounds he often squeezed in during his lunch hour.

We ended up loving everything about the restaurant. Seasons has a small outdoor terrace, while the cozy space inside has simple and kitschy décor. There are little wooden tables and chairs inside, and atop each table is a red-and-white-checkered cloth with a white candle. The walls are adorned with handmade crafts and framed posters and pictures of famous Himalayan sites—Mount Everest, the Boudhanath stupa in Kathmandu, and the memorial chorten in Thimphu.

The owner of Seasons is a delightfully witty Nepalese woman named Sandhya. She has tan skin a shade lighter than most Bhutanese and a round cherubic face. She speaks perfect English, as well as Hindi, Nepali, and Dzongkha. She has a half dozen men and women on her staff, but like most proprietors in Bhutan, Sandhya does much of the work herself. On one cool, rainy evening, Sandhya was running around the restaurant while doing everything: serving my two friends—Tempa, a man, and Tshering, a woman—and me; cooking our food; and sweeping the floor and busing dishes.

"Is the pizza better here or in New York?" asked Sandhya.

"No comparison," I said. "Your yak pizza is the best pizza I've ever had."

The pizza is so good for many reasons. The crust is deep, crisp, and light. The cheese and tomato sauce are perfectly blended to create a moist but not runny layer on top of the crust; and the toppings are succulent. With yak meat, Sandhya cuts inch-long slices and sautées them before laying them atop the pie. Seasons also has the best spaghetti (Bolognese was my favorite) and desserts in town; my top two sweets were the homemade apple tart (crispy on top, juicy inside) and tiramisu (fluffy and sweet).

THE BUSINESSES YOU find in Thimphu are similar to what you'd find in the rest of the world—restaurants, clothing stores, barbershops, butchers, bakeries, and groceries. But there are big differences when shopping in Bhutan. One is variety. There's just one movie theater, one real grocery store (though there are dozens of boutique food shops), and one post office in Thimphu, for example. Then there's the difference with what's inside the stores. Bhutanese butchers have no refrigeration systems and thus serve only truly fresh goods. The meats (predominantly chicken, beef, and yak) are sliced and diced in front of your eyes and carcasses hang on steel clips or sit on wooden planks, blood dripping and steam sometimes rising from them because they're so freshly killed. I'm not a foodie, but even my unsophisticated palate could tell the difference between the fresh chicken in Thimphu and the bland chicken in New York markets. Bhutanese bakeries, meanwhile, make fresh breads and pastries, which are surprisingly tasty and light despite the primitive ovens and limited availability of specialized ingredients. My favorite things at the bakeries were lemon tarts, apple pies, and éclairs.

While driving along the main road, I didn't see any street signs, so I asked Tashi what the road is called.

"It doesn't have a name," Tashi said. "We don't have names for streets and roads in Bhutan."

"So how do you know addresses?" I asked.

"We don't use addresses," he said. "We just know where things are."

Strange—a country without street names and addresses. "So when you send a letter, what do you write on the envelope?" I asked.

"You write the person's name and their hometown," Tashi replied. "Sometimes you also write their business or the section of town where they live. We do that because so many people have the same name."

"How does the mailman know where to go?" I asked.

"We don't have many mailmen," Tashi replied. "I go to the post office to get letters."

"What if you're giving directions?" I asked.

I couldn't fathom how a country could exist without something so basic as street names and addresses. Tashi, though, was unfazed and unaware of how strange his explanations seemed to me.

"We don't give directions," Tashi said. "We just know where to go."

WHILE STROLLING AROUND town, I recognized the barbershop where I'd gotten a haircut as a tourist in 2000. It's a minuscule shop, about 150 square feet. The barbers are Bangladeshi men who speak no English, which wasn't a problem because verbal communication isn't necessary when you're getting a crew cut. "Army," I said. I then held up my right hand and held the ends of my thumb and right forefinger very close together. The barber understood what that meant.

The shop has two barber chairs and two electric shaving-cream machines. The barbers prefer using industrial electric razors to cut hair, even with female customers, although during my time in the shop I noticed that the barbers can be cajoled into using scissors. The wood-plank walls are festooned with large mirrors surrounded by stickers of comic-book characters, a calendar from a Bhutanese cement company, and posters and magazine pages with buxom Bollywood actresses in short skirts, skintight shirts, and suggestive poses. Like it or not, pornography lives, even in Bhutan.

"Let's go in there," I said.

"It's not open," replied Tashi.

"Huh?" I said incredulously.

The door was closed, and when I looked closer, I noticed that nobody was inside.

"It's Wednesday," Tashi said. "The lower shops are closed."

I stared blankly, unable to comprehend the situation.

"All the shops on the lower side of the main road are closed on Wednesday," Tashi continued. "The shops here on the upper side of the road are closed on Tuesdays."

It was one of the most illogical things I'd ever heard. Tashi said, not very convincingly, that the closing days were a government-imposed tradition intended to force shopkeepers to take work breaks and to help with traffic congestion. I asked many more people about this peculiar tradition but nobody could give a concrete answer. (Now it's a moot point. In 2005, the government abolished the closing-day rule.)

"So let's go to a barber on the upper side of the road," I said.

Tashi looked puzzled. "I don't know any," he said. "I'll have to ask somebody." Tashi went into a store and spoke to a woman in Dzongkha, and he came out smiling. "She says there's a barber over there," he said, pointing to a road that intersected the main road about 100 yards away from us. We walked to the intersection and looked into every shop. There was no barber. Tashi asked another shopkeeper for help, but the man didn't know any barbers.

"Very strange," I said to nobody in particular. "It's the middle of a weekday afternoon and it's impossible to get a haircut."

Tashi wasn't bewildered. "Maybe we should get you a razor?" he said.

Tashi led me to Thimphu's only bona fide supermarket. Called Tashi (sometimes it seems like everybody and everything in Bhutan is named Tashi), it covers about 2,500 square feet and sits on the ground floor of the two-floor building surrounding Thimphu's main public square. There are wide aisles, little steel shopping carts, and computerized cash registers with bar code scanners on the counter.

There were a few different razors in the personal hygiene section.

"I like this one," said Tashi, holding a Gillette Mach2.

"Looks nice," I said. "But why is that better than the others?"

"I don't know," he said. "I've never used any of these razors. It just looks cool."

I took the Mach2 and a can of shaving cream to one of the two checkout counters. I recalled using my ATM card in Pokhara, an outpost in central Nepal, and I was hoping to see another technological feat now as the clerk scanned the items. No luck. She rang up the razor and shaving cream manually.

"Why didn't you use the scanner?" I asked.

The clerk stared blankly. I knew she understood English, but she was stone-dead silent. Finally she spoke. "Oh, we never use those machines," she said. "Nobody knows how they work."

Chapter 5

THE BAD NEWS BEARS
OF BHUTAN

Rudy Duran gave me a warning before I left for Bhutan. "Teaching big shots can be a challenge," he said. "They're men who like to be in charge. They don't always listen. So you often just have to smile and tell them how great they're doing, even if they don't listen and can't hit the ball."

Fortunately, the Bhutanese bigwigs were attentive pupils. I'd like to think that I played a big role in their success as students, but there were other factors at work. First, the Bhutanese golfers were desperate. Very desperate. The only pros who had ever been to Bhutan were an American and a Bangladeshi who had each made fleeting visits in the 1980s, leaving the Bhutanese to learn the game alone. Second, and perhaps more importantly, was my good timing: I arrived in Bhutan in the heart of the golf tournament season, and that only added to the desperation.

The Bhutanese Golf Federation organizes a dozen tournaments a year. All of them are in Thimphu, and most of Bhutan's hundred golfers play in every event. That means that some of the participants, mainly army officers stationed in the remote eastern parts of the kingdom, drive for up to two days to reach Thimphu.

I'm guessing that no other country has a perfect participation rate in tournaments, but the Bhutanese hackers love their golf. They also love to gamble and win prizes. At tournaments, many players engage in a bevy of betting pools, with the winners sometimes netting a couple hundred dollars. Official tournament booty is even more valuable, with prizes that include televisions, refrigerators, ovens, and stereos. There are even two tournaments that give away a car for first place.

The great thing about the Bhutanese tournaments is their egalitarian nature. Virtually every competitor has a chance to win the top prize, because it usually goes to the champion not of the gross division but of the net division. (There are two methods of scorekeeping in golf, gross and net. Gross is the raw score, or total number of strokes taken. The net score is calculated by taking the gross score and deducting a player's handicap; so a 24-handicapper who shoots 99 will have a net score of 75, but in a net event he would beat a 4-handicapper who shoots 85 and has a net score of 81.)

When I got to Bhutan, the big talk at Royal Thimphu was the Bhutan Open, scheduled for the end of September. I figured everybody was gung ho because they had the chance to win a national championship, but that wasn't the case. Most players had no chance to win the gross division, and even the guys with low handicaps who could score low enough to win the gross division had something bigger on their minds: the big-screen TV and hot-water heater that would be the top prizes in the net division.

It was a boon to my job because everybody wanted lessons. Things got so hectic on the lesson tee that I had to get a date book to keep track of appointments, but not even that kept things orderly. One overzealous player erased a name in my date book and replaced it with his name. When both men showed up for a lesson at the same time, I looked in my book and noticed the erased name and figured out what had happened but didn't say anything. I just chuckled and convinced the men to take a joint lesson.

ONE EVENING A few days before the open, the practice tee was abuzz and I was jumping back and forth between golfers while giving tips. My array of teaching gear and gizmos was spread around the tee, and it was fun to see how quickly the Bhutanese guys had grown to enjoy using the stuff. The balloon Frisbees were the most popular item, and during their first attempts at standing with each foot on a Frisbee and swinging, none of the players around the tee that night could swing without toppling off balance.

Each time somebody wobbled over, the rest of the guys cheered. The atmosphere was giddy, but the verve each man showed on the Frisbees made it clear that the Bhutanese golfers had big egos. Finally, Yougs remained in balance while hitting a shot. "You win the prize," I said.

"What's that?" said Yougs.

"A free lesson," I said.

Everybody clapped and laughed, and then quickly went back to hitting balls.

At about six-thirty P.M., Randy strolled down to the tee. When he arrived, a few guys stopped hitting, turned around, and began hooting in a slightly sarcastic tone. This was their way of acknowledging Randy's prowess.

"Way to go, champ!" one man yelled.

"Maybe in my next life I'll be able to beat you," another man said.

Randy chuckled. "I'm getting old," he said. "You might not need to wait that long."

"You da man," said Leki Dorji, a tour operator. "If I had your game, I'd be rich!" Leki then turned around and spit a wad of red betel nut juice onto the turf.

Betel is a bitter, thimble-size nut that people suck like candy because it's full of arecaine and arecoline, alkaloids that, like nicotine, give a good buzz. In Bhutan it seems as if everybody, including many kids, are addicted to betel nut and chew it several times a day. The habit crosses socioethnic boundaries: men and women, rich and poor, Buddhist and Hindu all chew betel nut. I saw yak herders in the nether reaches of the mountains, and High Court justices in Thimphu, happily chomping away.

There's a basic routine that betel nut chewers follow. They wrap the nuts in little green betel leaves, which come not from the betel palm tree but from the betel pepper plant, and then stick the concoction into one side of their mouth, like a cowboy chewing tobacco, and suck away for about fifteen minutes. The nut emits a residue that leaves your teeth, lips, and gums bright red. Throughout Bhutan, many streets, sidewalks, walking paths, and roads are covered with a red polka-dot pattern because of the residue that people have spit out.

Randy was one of the few Bhutanese who didn't chew betel nut; at least he didn't chew around me, and his mouth wasn't red from residue. One of Bhutan's most decorated golfers, he has won four Bhutan opens and made a hole in one twice, but his claim to fame is his role on the Bhutanese team that beat China at the 1986 Asian Games in Seoul, South Korea. China isn't what you'd call an enemy of Bhutan, but for a pacifist country such as Bhutan, China is the closest thing it has. Many Bhutanese are unhappy with China's takeover of Tibet, owing to the personal tragedies and the Buddhist historical treasures and monasteries that have been eviscerated, and the Bhutanese government has been arguing for years with China over the border between the two countries. "It's sad, sad, what the Chinese have done," a golfer told me one day.

At the Asian Games, the Bhutanese knew they had no realistic chance to finish first. But they had a tiny chance to beat China, whom they had never beaten in any sporting event. Winning against China would be as good as gold.

It was a fluke that Bhutan even sent a golf team to the '86 Asian Games. A year before the games, Benji (who else?!) had heard about the competition and felt it would be a good chance to garner some international goodwill and gauge how Bhutan's golfers rated on an international level. So he went to his friend the king. "I promised His Majesty that if he agreed to get behind the idea, we would finish in the top ten. My neck was on the line," Benji told me.

With the king's blessing, Benji contacted People to People Sports, a U.S.–based charity that sends coaches of various sports to needy countries. Within a short time, Carl Marinello, a golf professional from Florida, was on his way to Bhutan. Marinello is now teaching golf in Southern Pines, North Carolina, but his stint in Bhutan was the highlight of his career. "It was the most amazing thing I've experienced," Marinello told me. "I think about Bhutan and those guys every day."

BEFORE GETTING THE job, Marinello had never heard of Bhutan. He learned about the existence of the kingdom and the job in early 1986 in a job advertisement for People to People in a PGA of America bulletin. "I was forty years old and wanted to give something back to the game," said Marinello. "The ad also caught my eye because I'd always wanted to go to Africa, and I assumed Bhutan was there."

A couple of weeks after applying, Marinello got a phone call from People to People. He had an interview on the spot, and at the end of the phone call they offered him the job. There was one caveat: He had to leave in ten days, because they'd already purchased the plane tickets.

Marinello put down the receiver and looked at his wife, who shrugged her shoulders and smiled. Marinello said yes.

His head was whirling. Marinello was so nervous about his new job that he hardly slept during the four-day journey to Bhutan, which went through India and included two aborted attempts to land in Paro that forced the Druk Air jet back to Calcutta.

After landing, Marinello, by then pale and trembling with exhaustion, was whisked off to Thimphu. The first place he stopped at was Benji's chief justice chambers at the High Court. Marinello hadn't eaten or drank anything in twenty-four hours, and he barely got up the stairs. Just after entering the office, which was full of dignitaries wearing ghos, Marinello crumbled into a ball on the floor and passed out. "The next thing I knew, I was lying on a bed in a hotel with a bunch of Bhutanese men standing over me," Marinello recalled. "All I could think was, 'Great, Carl. Nice first impression.'"

Things got better. It was February, and the Asian Games weren't until August. Benji had selected ten of the country's best players; Marinello would train them all and select the top four to make the trip to South Korea for the tournament. None of the players could break 80 and only a few could break 90, but the men were dedicated and rejiggered their work schedules to attend practices at Royal Thimphu twice a day, seven days a week. "They were a ragtag group," said Marinello, "the 'Bad News Bears of Bhutan.'"

Marinello usually toiled alone with his charges at Royal Thimphu, but one day he had a big audience. "I looked up one afternoon and saw a long, thin band of maroon slowly gliding down a nearby mountainside. It looked like a huge snake," said Marinello. "As the maroon snake got closer, I realized it was a line of monks, maybe forty of them. After an hour, they marched right onto the golf course, stood stone silent behind the practice tee, and watched my guys hit balls."

Another day, Marinello had to cancel practice because the king played. Marinello was with Benji on the clubhouse steps when His Majesty arrived at Royal Thimphu, and the king walked past Marinello without saying a word. "He knew who I was, but he didn't even look at me," recalled Marinello. "On the first tee, he rolled down the top half of his gho—he had a golf shirt underneath—and teed off. The first fairway was lined with so many security guards, I turned to Benji and said, 'Jesus, he might be the only golfer on earth who has no chance of losing a ball.' A few days later, Benji told me that the king liked that line."

By April, Marinello had selected his four players: Lotey, Randy, Karma Y. Tenzing (an agent with the Bhutanese equivalent to the CIA), and Karma (Mindy) Tenzing (an officer in the Foreign Ministry). With financial backing from Royal Thimphu members, Marinello took them to train at the Royal Calcutta Golf Club in India for two months, and the team played thirty-six holes on most days in 100-plus-degree heat. They also enjoyed Calcutta's thriving nightlife. "Those Bhutanese guys took me everywhere, including to where the prostitutes worked, but we didn't do anything," said Marinello.

Really? Nothing?

"Nah, the guys usually wanted to go home early," said Marinello. "They wanted to work hard and impress the king."

After Calcutta, the team flew to Hong Kong with the financial support of a Chinese businessman, and then they jetted to Seoul, where another businessman lavished the golfers with sumptuous meals, golf at posh courses, and free use of a black Mercedes limousine. Finally August arrived, and the games began.

In the first round of the seventy-two-hole event with two dozen teams, the Bhutanese played better than Marinello expected, and everybody shot in the mid-80s. Marinello attributed the Bhutanese aptitude for golf to their aptitude for archery, the national sport. "Archery gives them the tunnel vision you need to hone in on a target," said Marinello. The Bhutanese continued their solid play, and after fifty-four holes they were in eleventh place, just five shots behind China.

In the final round, each Bhutanese fired the lowest score of his life. The team posted two rounds in the 70s and two in the 80s to help Bhutan leapfrog over China, besting them by six shots and finishing tenth overall. Tenth might not sound great, but the team's finish was a landmark event in Bhutanese sports history, and it reverberated in Bhutan somewhat like the U.S. ice hockey team's triumph over the USSR at the 1980 Winter Olympics did in America.

"It was surreal," said Marinello. "The Bhutanese were so damn happy, but nobody jumped or screamed. They just smiled and talked about the honor they felt for their country and their king."

IT WAS POURING. BUT you wouldn't have known that judging by the horde of golfers at Royal Thimphu. As another monsoonlike downpour pelted Thimphu, men were playing on the course and hitting at the practice tee, while I was doing a clinic for a dozen high schoolers (mostly boys, but a few girls) by the short-game practice area near the clubhouse. Back home, any course would be empty, but driving rain doesn't deter the Bhutanese. Or perhaps everybody just wanted to get ready for the Bhutan Open, rain be damned.

"I never thought of us as being tough," said Benji, whose bald scalp was wet as much with sweat as with rain as he was hitting balls on the range.

This morning, I'd been teaching Benji about the line of compression—imagine the clubhead is a bullet that fires down and into the golf ball. And now, hours later, he was still practicing, trying to remain in balance while trying to imagine himself compressing the ball with his club. "Imagine you're driving a hammer down into the ball at an almost 45-degree angle," I said.

"Good image," Benji said without looking up.

The kids I was teaching were equally excited about golf and unimpeded by the weather. I divided them into two groups of six. Each person from one group hit chips to the green, while somebody from the other group held a club next to his or her head, with the grip lightly touching the head. I had them do that to keep the person steady while swinging. David Leadbetter does this drill all the time with tour players, and it is very effective with amateurs, too.

The kids enjoyed the drill because it offered room to play games. One boy tapped the grip against the head of a girl as she was hitting.

"Ouch," she said.

"That didn't hurt," the boy said. "I hardly bopped you."

I called the kids into a circle around me in the middle of the putting green. The rain had slowed to a steady drizzle. "How'd you like to win a TV?" I said.

Everybody raised a hand. "How can we do that?" one boy asked.

"Pretty soon, they're having the Bhutan Open," I said. "If you all practice really hard, you can play in the Bhutan Open sometime. Maybe next year. And they give away great prizes. TVs, stereos, even Druk Air tickets to Bangkok."

"Can we play this year?" a girl asked.

"You can't even hit a drive," a boy next to her said.

I enoyed the good-spirited needling the kids always gave each other during clinics. That was one of the most fun parts of teaching them.

It was dusk, but I looked down to the range, which was 100 yards away, on the other side of the first fairway, and it was still full of golfers. Soon Randy walked up from the range to watch the kids in my group. They were back to the balance drill, flopping little chips as another person held a club to their heads to steady them.

Most of the kids had never touched a club before I arrived, and now they'd been to only a few clinics. Already, though, all of them were making decent contact with these little shots.

"Think there's a Tiger here?" Randy asked me.

"Your kids have the same natural talent as kids in America and everyplace else," I said. "Just give them the same resources and you'll be watching them on TV someday."

"That is a dream I hope I live to see," said Randy.

Chapter 6

SPEAKING OUT: THE BHUTANESE
WILL BE HEARD

CARRIE AND I were so keen to move to Bhutan largely because of the chance to live amid and explore the kingdom's vast expanses of beauty and cultural riches. But so far, after a few weeks, we hadn't done much of anything. We hadn't taken a hike or even a little walk through the woods. We hadn't visited a monastery or been to the spiffy new textile museum in Thimphu. Aside from the golf course, some shopping, and an occasional jog along the Thimphu River, Carrie and I had hardly gone anywhere.

You could say we'd been holed up in a house. But I see it differently. We'd had no reason to leave Benji's house and explore because Benji's house was the most fun place to be in Bhutan.

Carrie and I spent much of our time in the house just sitting in the living room with Benji while he regaled us with stories, each more fascinating and unbelievable than the last. Smoking marijuana with CIA agents in India. Doing karaoke with Mick Jagger in Thimphu. Sipping tea with Sophia Loren in London. Having lunch with President Bush (the father) in Buenos Aires. One of his greatest yarns, which changed slightly from one telling to the next, was about his experience at the cremation ceremony in Delhi for Indira Gandhi, the Indian prime minister who was assassinated on October 31, 1984.

"I went with His Majesty, mainly to serve as his bodyguard," Benji said during dinner one night. "We were at some hotel in Delhi with with all the other dignitaries. You know, Margie Thatcher and Princess Anne and the rest of them. So on the day of the cremation, we're all riding this rickety bus to the ceremony. It had wood plank floors, no air-conditioning, and we were bumping up and down."

Benji pushed back his dining chair and began rising up and down to imitate the bus ride.

"Can you imagine?" he continued. "Margie and the rest of them must've been horrified."

Carrie was cracking up. I was laughing, too. I particularly liked Benji's emphasis on using first names.

"So we get to the place [Shakti Sthal, the site in Delhi where the cremation was held] and the king and I are sitting next to the president of some country."

"Do you remember who it was?" I asked.

"Some president," Benji said nonchalantly. "Well, I had my gun at my side, in my gho. I was there, after all, to protect His Majesty. I think my gun must've been rubbing against this president, because suddenly he turned to me and asked, 'Who are you?'"

Benji paused and began laughing. He continued, "I told him, 'I am the duke of Gangtey.' [Gangtey is the name of a palace in Paro where Benji's family used to reside.] The king started cracking up, and the president didn't say another word."

As much as we loved being with Benji, we didn't see him nearly as much as we wanted to. When it was dark out, he was usually at a party or a bar. Meanwhile, when the sun was up he was either asleep, recovering from his wild shenanigans, playing golf, or in his bedroom watching cricket and doing crossword puzzles.

But Benji's house was still a fun place to be even without the master of ceremonies. Claudia was especially happy; one of her favorite places in the house was the bathroom. She was still in diapers so she didn't use the toilet, but I bathed her in the bathroom. There wasn't a tub, and we didn't haul one of those plastic baby tubs to Bhutan. Instead, I washed Claudia in a little red bucket placed on the floor of the shower stall. Today, Claudia could only fit one leg in the bucket, but back in 2002, as a nine-month-old, she could easily sit in the bucket and she liked it so much that bathtime often lasted for thirty minutes.

MY FAVORITE PLACE in Benji's house was the lone bedroom on the ground floor. It belonged to Tashi Namgay, a high school junior and the youngest of Benji's three sons. Benji's eldest son, about thirty-five, was an actor and model who lived in Mumbai, India. (Of course, Benji had a mind-jarring story about him: He was dating Sushmita Sen, winner of the 1994 Miss Universe pageant and the first Indian to take that crown.) His middle son, about thirty, was the chief bodyguard for the crown prince.

Tashi Namgay's bedroom had Bon Jovi and World Wrestling Entertainment posters on the walls, blue jeans and T-shirts strewn on the floor, and tubes of hair gel and dirty combs on the wooden dresser. There wasn't a bed, just a mattress and box spring on the floor. There was a color TV, and it was almost always on when Tashi Namgay was home, but Tashi watched only MTV and Nickelodeon, even though the cable TV service offered forty-five channels.

Being addicted to TV is common among Bhutanese youth. Soon after TV was legalized in 1999, children across the country, even in some of the remotest areas, became glued to their new tubes. One survey from 2003 found that children in Bhutan's urban areas watched an average of twelve hours of television per week—a lot less than the twenty-eight hours per week American children average, but still a huge amount, considering that just a short time ago Bhutanese children watched no TV at all.

While no conclusive studies have been done to prove that TV has harmed Bhutan's kids, there is lots of anecdotal evidence. One problem has been a rise in violence among youth, which many Bhutanese believe is caused at least partly by children watching professional wrestling. Schoolteachers also often complain that students are less focused in the classroom because they're tired from staying up at night to watch TV. A more severe problem with youth has been a rise in drug use, including alcohol and marijuana, while glue sniffing exists as well. During the first eleven months of 2003, 209 people had been arrested in Thimphu for drug abuse, and 97 of them were students. Police said those arrested represented just a small fraction of the total drug users.

Television didn't seem to have any terrible influence on Tashi Namgay, except that he spent countless hours supine on his bed watching the tube. Carrie and I also spent many hours in Tashi Namgay's room, shooting the breeze with him and his best friends, Nienzie (a female cousin) and Kesang (a male friend), and watching TV. Nienzie and Kesang, both classmates, were in Tashi Namgay's room almost every day after school and often on the weekends. Kesang also slept over quite often.

TASHI NAMGAY, NIENZIE, and Kesang were not typical Bhutanese youth. They were children of privilege, representing a tiny fraction of the population, and thus they had access to luxuries including golf and foreign travel, and they were also doted on by servants. (Kesang was from a middle-class family, but he spent so much time at Tashi's house that he was almost like a brother and thus enjoyed many of the things that Tashi did.)

On the other end of the social spectrum were the caddies at Royal Thimphu. All boys ranging from ten to sixteen years old, the caddies, mostly from poor families, had parents who were farmers, chauffeurs, domestic servants, or shopkeepers. The differences between rich and poor are dramatic in Bhutan, as they are elsewhere. For example, most of the caddies had never been outside of Thimphu, they wore ratty clothes that were usually soiled, and they walked everywhere. Some caddies walked for over an hour from their homes to the course. Meanwhile, Tashi frequently took vacations to Thailand and India, he donned the same jeans, polo shirts, and Nikes (real, not knockoffs) I wore as a child and he never walked anyplace. He either drove himself around in his father's Land Cruiser (not having a driver's license didn't seem to matter) or he got a ride from a friend.

One thing the rich and poor kids had in common was a lack of things to do. In America, it seems like there are a million and one activities for children, beginning at a young age. Not in Bhutan. I haven't seen the whole country, but in all the places I've visited in Bhutan I've seen just one playground, in Thimphu, and that was decrepit and unused. Most cities and villages have at least one big sports field, but the fields tend to be uneven and poorly maintained, with a lot more rocks and dirt than grass. The schools tend to provide very few extracurriculars to complement classroom studies, while outside of the school system there is also a dearth of organized activities. I came across a few programs for kids in Thimphu, including tae kwon do and tennis, but these were all privately run and too expensive for the average citizen.

The result is that kids are pretty much left to themselves to create their own amusements, which they do in very creative ways. When I arrived, I saw the caddies at Royal Thimphu using bent rebar and Coke bottles (yes, like Lee Trevino did as a boy) to hit balls around the practice putting green in the evenings. To play soccer, I saw many children in different parts of the country using balls made from wads of tape and paper. It's not that all the kids are poor. There's just very little activity and equipment, whether it be sports, music, or art, for them to use.

That's a big reason why Benji pushed Tashi Namgay and his friends to attend my youth clinics at Royal Thimphu. I was pleased that the kids genuinely enjoyed the clinics and excelled at golf, especially the girls, because girls get much less attention than boys in the few organized athletic programs that exist in Bhutan.

One particular evening, we were watching a young people's game show on Nickelodeon and discussing how things had changed since the TV ban was lifted in 1999. "Was it fair that the government banned TV and the Internet before 1999?" I asked.

"Some rules are good," said Nienzie. "It's good for the country."

"But is it good for somebody to censor what people can have?" I asked.

"There are some rules the government just makes," said Nienzie. "They tell us we have to wear our national dress when we go to the dzong, and we don't object because it shows respect and tradition. We call that *driglam namzhe*. That means discipline. So before we weren't really complaining about not having TV. But now if they told us we couldn't have TV, everybody would be opposed."

I shifted the conversation to a broader but related topic: why the Bhutanese seemed to have little inclination toward debating issues in public. When I asked why there is so little public criticism and analysis of the government and other institutions and rules, Kesang replied, "People feel hesitant. They are afraid."

"What could happen?" I asked.

"Nothing," said Kesang.

Comments like Kesang's revealed the unusual situation in Bhutan regarding public debate and free speech. Bhutan doesn't have any laws prohibiting free speech—individually, in the media, or anyplace else. But the caste system and remnants of feudalism have created a society that until very recently has been devoid of unfettered media and a citizenship willing to speak its mind in public. The newspaper *Kuensel* has been around since 1972 and is still owned partly by the government, which might be why the paper rarely criticizes public officials and does not do much investigative journalism. That, however, is not always for a lack of desire.

But Bhutan's radical governmental changes seem to have ushered in the beginning of a new era. The Bhutanese are becoming much more vocal, especially in public, and the media is expanding. By the end of 2006, two additional newspapers had started publication in Bhutan, and the Internet was teeming with blogs and chat forums in which Bhutanese were bluntly engaging in debates that just a couple of years ago would have been taboo to discuss in any public forum: whether marijuana should be legalized, whether capital punishment should be reinstated, and whether AIDS is more widespread in Bhutan than the official figures suggest.

Clearly the Bhutanese are no longer afraid to express themselves in public and challenge authority. No stronger proof of the radical change exists than what occurred in 2006 during the series of town hall meetings His Majesty and the crown prince held around the country to introduce the constitution and new government plans to the people and solicit their opinions. In years past, people would have sat stoically while the king and crown prince spoke, and perhaps politely applauded them. Nobody would have dared to ask a question or make a comment, even if invited to speak by His Majesty or the crown prince. But at the 2006 town hall meetings, hoi polloi spoke often and with shocking candor during the question-and-answer sessions at the end of the speeches. At the first meeting, when a few thousand Bhutanese gathered in Thimphu, one man asked the king whether the new constitution should have a provision regarding the number of wives future kings could have.

Asking such a question would have been heretical in the old Bhutan. But democracy is coming, and the many voices of Bhutan will be heard. Especially the young voices, which is why I spent so much time talking to Tashi and his friends. They represent the newer, Westernized generation of Bhutanese, and the success of the king's grand transformative plan will depend on these nascent minds, many of which have been influenced as much, if not more, by external forces (the Internet and TV, for example) as by internal ones, including Buddhism and the king.

AT THE END of our conversation, I asked the kids if they felt it was okay for the king to have four wives. Nienzie piped up right away. She was laughing.

"He's the *king*," she said.

"Would you want your husband to have four wives?" I asked.

"No way!" said Nienzie. "I wouldn't want to share somebody I love with other women. Yuck!"

"If the king asked you to be one of his four wives, would you do it?" I asked.

"You'd do it," said Tashi. He and Kesang were laughing.

Nienzie wasn't laughing. "I wouldn't do it," she replied. "My grandmother sometimes tries to persuade me, my sister, and some cousins of mine to marry this *tulku*, the reincarnation of a big lama. He's in his midthirties. He already has a wife. I've said, 'We're educated now. We don't do that.'"

"What about the crown prince?" I asked. (The prince, Jigme Khesar Namgyal Wangchuck, was 22 years old in 2002, and unmarried. His father married in 1979, around the time of his twenty-fourth birthday.) "What'll he do?"

"He has many girlfriends," said Nienzie. "He's trying hard to do the right thing."

"What will that be?" I said.

"I don't know," Nienzie said. "That I seriously don't know."

Chapter 7

LAMAS, ELTON JOHN, AND
HORSE POOP

M Y EYES WERE agape when I first saw Lama Tsultrim
Dorji. He'd come to meet me at the street corner by his
apartment building in Thimphu. At the request of Palden Tshering, my friend from Royal Thimphu, Lama Tsultrim had invited
me over to give me a formal introduction to Buddhism.

Palden told me it would be okay to laugh at the lama. "Everybody cracks up inside when they meet him," Palden said. "Out
of respect, most people refrain from laughing out loud, but the
lama doesn't care if you do. He's mellow and won't be insulted.
He knows he looks funny with those wild glasses."

Funny? No, hilarious. Imagine a potbellied, forty-five-year-old
monk chomping on gum and wearing a flowing maroon robe and
faux leather sandals. Then imagine that monk having a shiny bald
scalp, plump red cheeks, and a sarcastic grin. Sounds like Santa
Claus and the Dalai Lama all in one, right? But there's more.
Imagine the monk wearing a pair of Elton John–style sunglasses,
the shades with preposterously thick black frames and huge round
lenses with a neon orange hue.

When I got out of my taxi and caught my first glimpse of

Lama Tsultrim, who was across the street from me, I started to laugh. Acknowledging my chuckles, he said, "I can tell, you *like* the glasses. They're cool. No?"

How do you reply to a reincarnated monk who says *that*?

"Very cool," I blurted. "You look like Elton John."

Lama Tsultrim smiled again. "Many people say that, especially foreigners. I do not know Mr. John, but he must be a good man."

My mind wandered. I imagined Lama Tsultrim seated at a black Steinway, tip-tapping the keyboard and swaying from side to side while crooning "Crocodile Rock." Then Lama Tsultrim said, "Follow me." He turned around and guided me across the street, along a twisty dirt path and up a little hill toward his building. I scratched my head. Was Lama Tsultrim for real? Was everything I've read about Buddhism true? Or was there a major disconnect between the image of Buddhism and reality?

Whatever the case, this was clearly going to be one of the biggest thrills of my life.

LAMA TSULTRIM IS one of the approximately six thousand monks in Bhutan. Unlike most of those monks, Lama Tsultrim is not part of the official monkhood, which is the national system of monks that has a formal hierarchy and is supported by the government. Lama Tsultrim grew up in that system, but he left it as an adult because he didn't feel he could make as much spiritual progress in the formal monkhood, which would have required him to spend too much time doing chores around monasteries.

The formal monkhood is governed by its leader, the *je khenpo*.

Until the Bhutanese monarchy was established in 1907, the je khenpo ruled over not only the monkhood but also was a coruler of the kingdom who worked in tandem with the top government officials. In recent times the je khenpo's official powers outside of the monkhood have been drastically curtailed, but he is still a mighty figurehead, revered almost as much as the king, whom he serves as a trusted adviser. Below the je khenpo are four *lonpons*, or masters, and together this quintet governs the affairs of the monkhood in Bhutan.

A revered monk known as Guru Rinpoche brought Buddhism to Bhutan in the eighth century. Legend has it that Guru Rinpoche immigrated to Bhutan from Tibet by flying on the back of a female tiger over the strip of high peaks that separate the two countries. He arrived in a deep valley 5 miles north of what is now Paro and spent three months meditating in a cave 3,000 feet above the valley floor on a sheer rock cliff. In 1692, a sprawling monastery called Taktshang was built on the site of the cave to honor Guru Rinpoche. Now known as Tiger's Nest, Taktshang has become Bhutan's most famous monastery, partly because of its religious significance and partly because its setting on the side of a cliff seems to defy physics. The Bhutanese show their devotion to Guru Rinpoche by putting his iconic image—a large, lamaesque man sitting Indian-style with a gleaming golden face—right next to Lord Buddha's in almost every religious shrine in the kingdom.

In the seventeenth century, a powerful leader from Tibet, Shabdrung Ngawang Namgyal, immigrated to Bhutan and became the kingdom's leader, and while consolidating his power he made a major religious change by establishing the state religion as the Drukpa Kagyu lineage of Buddhism. Instead of banishing the Nyingma sect that had been established by Guru

Rinpoche, Shabdrung allowed it to be practiced in the central and eastern parts of the country.

Buddhism completely pervades everyday life, politics, and culture in Bhutan. Most buildings—private dwellings, stores, gas stations, and government offices—are festooned with Buddhist motifs on the outside and have religious artwork such as thangkas (paintings) inside. Two striking examples are the primary court-room at the High Court, and the National Assembly Hall, both in Thimphu and both decorated in a kaleidoscope of red, blue, green, and white Buddhist symbols and scenes. Virtually every home in Bhutan has a prayer altar and Buddhist artwork. Pic-tures of reincarnated lamas hang from rearview mirrors in cars, while stupas and chortens are as widespread in cities and villages as telephone booths are in New York. Monks officiate at virtu-ally every significant ceremony, from naming babies to wed-dings to funerals. At the start of important events, whether it's an archery tournament, a fashion show, or the groundbreaking cer-emony for a new building, there's almost always a monk to con-fer blessings and prayers.

The Bhutanese are the most religious people, as a nation, I've ever seen, and their devotion to Buddhism is admirable. But the pervasiveness of Buddhism in Bhutan leaves many of its citizens feeling a bit guilty that they don't fulfill 100 percent of the reli-gion's ideals and practices.

One such person was Leki Dorji, a tour company and restau-rant owner and golfer who plays at Royal Thimphu. Leki regu-larly prays, consults monks for key decisions, and has monks officiate Buddhist rituals for all important family and personal cer-emonies, such as births, deaths, and the christening of a new home. But Leki, who has a brother who is a reincarnated lama based in Taiwan and has a large following in Asia, Europe, and the

U.S., aspires to be an even more devout Buddhist. Well, at least part of him does. "If I were to really follow Buddhism, I'd have to live like a monk," said Leki. "Religion is like golf. Lots of people don't follow all the rules. To truly follow Buddhism, you can't kill anything, for example, but I love fishing. This kind of thing mixes me up."

BEFORE HE CLOSED the front door of his apartment, Lama Tsultrim asked how I like my tea. "With sugar and milk?" he said.

"A little milk," I told him, and he brought it to me in a beige ceramic coffee mug with a handle. The mug reminded me of the dish set I'd bought at Kmart for my first apartment in New York fifteen years ago, which wasn't surprising. Those dishes from Kmart were probably made in China, and most of the dishes sold in Bhutan are imported from China (and routed through Tibet).

Lama Tsultrim's four-room apartment was in one of the plethora of institutional looking concrete apartment houses around Thimphu. The buildings looked like spartan college dorms built in the 1970s. Lama Tsultrim's abode had high ceilings and was comfortably furnished. Like many middle-class dwellings in Thimphu, his home had a sofa and cushioned chairs in the living room, a bed and dresser in the main bedroom, and a dining table in the kitchen. The second bedroom had been converted into a prayer room with a floor-to-ceiling prayer altar adorned with butter lamps, plastic flowers, palm-size metallic bowls with candles, beaded necklaces, and other Buddhist good-luck mementoes. Several thangkas with Buddhist folktales and images of iconic figures including Guru Rinpoche hung on the walls.

Lama Tsultrim was born in Tibet. In 1959 he was four years

old when his family immigrated to Bhutan by foot as one of the thousands of families who fled Tibet. As soon as the Communists took control of China in 1949, they began a campaign to wrest control of Tibet and replace Tibetan history and culture with Chinese history and culture. For a decade the Tibetans staged a resistance using diplomacy and military force, but by early 1959 it was clear that the Tibetans were no match for the mighty Chinese. In March 1959, the Dalai Lama fled to India after the Chinese quashed a violent Tibetan uprising in Lhasa, the capital, and the Dalai Lama's departure caused a mass exodus of his countrymates. "My parents were very afraid of the Chinese and wanted to go to a peaceful place," Lama Tsultrim said. "My mother carried me on her back the whole way to Bhutan, even over the high passes."

THE BHUTANESE MONKHOOD has undergone a dramatic reduction over the past few decades, shrinking by tens of thousands. One sure sign of the monkhood's declining role is the fact that it's rare for families to send the firstborn son into the monkhood unless a family is poor and either can't afford to support the child or send him to school, or both. (Schools are free in Bhutan, but families must pay for uniforms and books.) Indeed, many of the men at Royal Thimphu are eldest sons but I know of just one club member who was a monk, and he left the monkhood after some years and now owns a convenience store in Thimphu. Years ago, though, firstborn sons were almost always sent into the monkhood for two reasons: education (monasteries had the only schools) and honor (it was a way to show respect to the deities and gain merit).

So it was no surprise that, as he was the first son in his family, Lama Tsultrim's parents sent him to a monastery in Paro when he was six years old. At the monastery he was given the name Karma Kunzang Tempa. He learned to read and write, and he showed such preternatural understanding of Buddhism and such devotion to his prayers that at age eleven he was sent on a pilgrimage for several weeks to a Buddhist monastery in India.

By fourteen, Lama Tsultrim was appointed to the group of monks at his monastery who went into the community to perform prayers and officiate at ceremonies. His rise in the ranks took another major leap forward when at age eighteen he requested and was given permission to do a major meditation retreat, which in Bhutan lasts for three years, three months, and three days, and is a key stepping-stone to becoming a lama. Most monks spend their entire lives toiling in monasteries, where they pray and perform rituals, but also spend considerable time cleaning and doing other maintenance work. Lama Tsultrim didn't want that to be his fate. "I had higher aspirations," he said. "I wanted to become a window to the higher world for my people."

So for the next twelve hundred days, Lama Tsultrim lived alone in a single room in the upper Thimphu Valley. His room had a toilet, a sink with a cold-water tap, a burner for cooking fueled by propane, but that was it. He slept on a mat on the concrete floor, shaved without a mirror, washed with a bucket and cold water, and had no electricity. Without any money, he relied on his parents to routinely bring him a solitary monk's staples: rice, biscuits, noodles, tea, butter lamps, incense. But they couldn't speak to or see their son; they had to leave the supplies at the door to his room.

Lama Tsultrim's days were all virtually the same. Wake up at three A.M.; wash his hands and face; meditate until six-thirty;

have a biscuit and tea and maybe some rice; meditate from eight to one-thirty P.M.; prepare and eat lunch (rice, a biscuit, maybe some noodles); nap for thirty minutes; meditate from three to five; have some tea and rice for dinner; meditate until ten P.M., and then go to sleep. Was that a lonely time? "A little in the first and second weeks," said Lama Tsultrim. "But then it was very peaceful, very quiet, very successful."

As I sat listening to Lama Tsultrim, I thought about how at that moment there were dozens, perhaps hundreds, of monks in Bhutan, and many more around the world, amid their extended stints of solitary meditation. I thought about Thoreau and Walden Pond, about Tiger Woods sweating alone on the driving range at Isleworth, about Tim Berners-Lee toiling in his lab on the way to inventing the World Wide Web. Perhaps mankind's quest for peace and happiness in the West, where we're so focused on material gains and group bonding, is not the road we should follow? Maybe we should take a lesson from the meditating monks?

Based on Lama Tsultrim's enormously positive memories of his retreats, meditating monks might be some of the happiest people on earth, and some of the most productive. "I was so busy all the time, because I had so much to learn, to study. Every day I prayed for the health and happiness of the world of sentient beings," said Lama Tsultrim.

Lama Tsultrim hasn't stopped praying. He did a second three-year, three-month, and three-day retreat, and was soon thereafter anointed as a lama, which is a monk who is especially learned and spiritual. As a lama, he left the main monk body because he felt he could make more spiritual progress and share Buddhism with more people working on his own, essentially as a freelancer.

What does a freelance lama do?

Some of them leave Bhutan and open meditation centers abroad. They develop a group of followers who either visit them at their meditation centers or bring them to their homes to guide them in meditation sessions. These followers typically pay the monks for their services, and the payments, while usually not set to a specific rate, sometimes involve many thousands of dollars a year.

Lama Tsultrim told me that he never wanted to move away from Bhutan. "My heart is here," he said.

Now, he spends at least six hours a day, seven days a week, meditating and reciting Buddhist prayers in his prayer room. He earns money by praying for people and performing ceremonies. "Fifty, one hundred dollars, they pay what they want," Lama Tsultrim told me. "I have no set fees."

LAMA TSULTRIM LED me to his prayer room. He smoothly bent down and prostrated for several minutes in front of the altar, chanting prayers in a gentle, mellifluous tone. I couldn't help thinking about the scene in *Caddyshack* where Bill Murray, playing Carl Spackler, a golf course superintendent, delivers a soliloquy about caddying for a lama playing a round of golf in the Himalayas.

As I watched Lama Tsultrim sitting up then down, up then down, I imagined that he was the lama for whom Spackler caddied. There, in my dream, is Lama Tsultrim in his red robe and sandals standing on the precipice of a cliff about to tee off at his eighteenth and final hole of the round. Snowcapped mountains surround him. The only sound is the whirling wind. He's playing alone. Spackler is standing near the lama, his hand holding up the lama's bag on the ground between them. Then I recall one of Murray's more riotous lines from the movie:

> So we finish the eighteenth and he's gonna stiff me.
> And I say, "Hey, Lama, hey, how about a little some-
> thing, you know, for the effort, you know." And he
> says, "Oh, uh, there won't be any money, but when
> you die, on your deathbed, you will receive total con-
> sciousness." So I got that goin' for me, which is nice.

My golf buddies back home in the States and I have repeated that line so many times that it's etched into my memory. Lama Tsultrim had never played golf; indeed, monks are supposed to shun sports, although many young monks play soccer during their free time. But I figured this was a perfect time to ask for a kernel of wisdom from a real-life lama.

"What's the best path to happiness?" I asked.

Lama Tsultrim smiled, pausing to think before replying. "In Bhutan, our country is so developed, it is hard to be happy," he said. "People are becoming rich, but they are not peaceful. They have only outside peace, but you need inside peace to be happy. Bhutanese are too busy, too much suffering and worry-ing now."

Lama Tsultrim paused and looked out the window. His smile was still beaming. "It is like, you know, the horse," he said.

I was lost. "Huh?" I said.

"The horse eats, then, you know," said Lama Tsultrim while wrapping his right arm behind his back and pointing a finger at his buttocks. "What do you call that in America?"

"Poop?" I replied.

"Yes!" Lama Tsultrim said with genuine excitement. "Our peace now is like the horse poop. After the sun dries it, the poop is nice outside, but inside it is gooey, a mess. That is like Bhutan. Outside, Bhutan is beautiful, but inside it is not."

How do you reply to a reincarnated monk who says *that*? "I understand," I replied.

I looked at my watch. It was three-thirty P.M. and I had to be at Royal Thimphu for a kids' clinic at four o'clock. "I hope you'll understand, but I must leave," I said as I stood up and picked up my backpack. "I've got to teach some kids."

"Teach?" said Lama Tsultrim.

I thought he knew what I was doing in Bhutan, but apparently he didn't. "I'm the golf pro," I said.

"Oh, that must be a good game," said Lama Tsultrim. Did he really not know about golf?

"Have you heard of Tiger Woods?" I asked.

Lama Tsultrim and I were standing. He picked up the plate of butter cookies from the coffee table. "Please, take some cookies."

I took two.

My question didn't register. So I asked once more.

"*Tiger?*" said Lama Tsultrim. He looked puzzled and bashful.

I bowed and shook hands with Lama Tsultrim. "Thank you, thank you," I said. "I am most grateful for your time."

I scampered down the stairway, along the dirt path, and back to the road. While walking through town and back to the golf course, I couldn't stop smiling. I'll never forget the words that came from Lama Tsultrim's mouth or the curious look on his face when I asked if he knew of Tiger Woods. It was so refreshing to meet people who were still immune to Western society and modernization.

During the half-hour walk to Royal Thimphu, I kept picturing Lama Tsultrim standing in his apartment by the front door and saying, "*Tiger?*"

I have a hunch that even Tiger Woods would be pleased.

Chapter 8

THE BHUTAN OPEN

IT WAS A Thursday, two days before the Bhutan Open, and Randy and I were alone on the practice tee. Randy had brought the open's trophy to Royal Thimphu so the club could display it in the clubhouse and have it on hand to give to the winner on Sunday afternoon. The trophy was a foot-high gold-plated cup mounted on a mahogany base. Randy put the trophy down on the grass and began swinging his pitching wedge.

"How's my swing look?" Randy asked.

In the backswing, Randy was swaying his chest and hips away from the target. In the follow-through, he was swaying toward the target. I filmed him on my video camera and showed Randy the swing in slow motion. "Wow," he said. "I'm swimming around like a fish. That's no good."

I recalled a drill I had taught some of the kids at Royal Thimphu. The teacher stands opposite to the student and holds a club in the air, parallel to the ground, with the end of the grip resting against the target side of the player's head. This is one of the most popular drills on the pro tours. Randy took a few swings as I stood there with the grip against his head, and he stopped swaying almost immediately. "Feels so solid," said Randy. "Like I'm a tree trunk. Very good."

"Anything I can do to help with the tournament?" I asked.

"How do you set up the pins in America?" Randy asked.

Randy was referring to the method used to select the hole locations for competitions. "I think the way they do it on tour is to divide the holes into three groups—easy, medium, and hard—and choose six hole locations in each category," I said. "You guys have only nine holes, so you could do three sets of three."

"That sounds good. Could you do that with Tshering, our course manager, for both days of the tournament?" Randy asked.

"Sure," I replied. "When?"

"Tomorrow morning."

AT SEVEN-THIRTY THE next morning, Royal Thimphu was covered with glimmering dew. As Tshering and I walked down the first fairway, we left a trail of parallel footprints that reminded me of when I used to caddie for the Dewsweepers, the foursome at Westchester Country Club who always teed off at six-thirty A.M. on weekend mornings. When we got to the first green at Royal Thimphu, a tiny and flat putting surface, I was surprised to see a plethora of itty-bitty mushrooms.

"You have chemicals to kill them in America," said Tshering. "I wish we could get such things in Bhutan."

Tshering, a lithe man with muscular arms who was in his midthirties, squatted down into a baseball catcher's stance, and I squatted next to him. "Look at the green, we have so many different grasses," Tshering said.

I looked closely and noticed the many shapes and subtle shades of green among the blades of grass. I'd never looked so closely at a putting green, which resembled the surface of a sponge with so many subtle permutations.

Tshering continued. "There are some diseased roots, too, mixed in. But there's nothing we can do. We must live with these things in Bhutan."

"But the greens still roll smoothly, so why are you concerned?" I asked.

"Soon the grass will die if we don't remove the mushrooms, the bad roots, and some of the bad grasses," Tshering said. "It is always a battle, and the members get angry if the greens are not good."

Tshering's concern for the greens and his trepidation about pleasing the members aren't unique. Course superintendents around the world walk on eggshells working under the fine microscope of their club's members, and clubs often fire supers when course conditions are anything less than pristine. It doesn't matter if the greens wilt or the fairways become sparse because of a drought or a pest. Golfers, especially country club golfers, are often more demanding with the staff at their clubs than they are with their own children. It was amusing to see this attitude in Bhutan, too.

Tshering and I walked down into the gentle swale behind the first green. The grass in the swale was shaved very low, just a bit higher than the grass on the green. "Perhaps it's too low," I said. "Now there's nothing to stop balls from running down the swale and into the thick fescue and bushes behind it."

Tshering looked flustered. "But the members want everything so challenging. They want this course to be as hard as Augusta. I'd like to please the members by cutting grass at different

levels in the roughs, like they do in America. But that's not possible. We have just one mowing machine that cuts one height,
and even that is always breaking down."

I suggested that Tshering put the pin in the back middle of
the first green, but he disagreed. "The members want it over
there," he said, pointing to the front of the green, which sits
next to a concrete pool. All but one of the water hazards at
Royal Thimphu are concrete. They used to be natural, but it
was too hard to find balls in the ponds, and balls are so hard to
come by in Bhutan that the club decided to go with concrete.

"The problem now is different," said Tshering. "The balls
sometimes roll into the drainpipes and clog them."

The green at the par-4 second hole sits near the middle of
the course, and from there you can see all nine holes. As I gazed
around the course, I saw men and women in traditional dress on
their hands and knees clipping grass with scissors around greens
and sweeping grass off tees with brooms. The tools and methods
were primitive, but the results were not. As we walked around,
I noticed that the fringes were neatly cropped and the tees were
immaculate.

The seventh hole is a 340-yard par 4 that climbs steeply uphill
from the tee to the green and bends slightly from left to right.
Between the tee and the fairway are 100 yards with scruffy grass
and a big pond, and then there's waist-high rough along the entire right side of the fairway. As Tshering and I walked up the
fairway, he told me about the Japanese golf course company
owned by a tycoon named Mr. Onishi that had renovated Royal
Thimphu a decade ago for free. Some members had bragged to
me about the renovation, noting that the modified hole routing
and course condition were both vastly improved, but Tshering
had a less sanguine opinion. "They didn't do a good job,"

Tshering said. "They just moved dirt and put seed on top of that, and then they let people begin playing too early. The grass never had time to take root. Also, they never installed drainage pipes or an irrigation system, and now we have many problems with big puddles after the rains."

The eighth hole is a 200-yard par 3 that drops sharply downhill. I normally hit a 2-iron from that distance, but here I use a 5-iron because of the severe downhill combined with the altitude. By the green, I saw one of the half dozen full-time workers on Tshering's maintenance crew. He was wearing a faded gho, dirty sweatpants, a baseball cap, and plastic knee-high work boots, and he was pushing an electric mower across the green. The man was about my age, but his skin was severely weather-beaten, deeply tanned, and full of thick, long wrinkles, like those I'd seen on farmers during my treks into the Bhutanese wilderness.

As I watched the man walk back and forth across the green, I heard beneath the purring of the mower's motor the din of monks chanting in a nearby monastery and saw a couple of cows munching grass on the lower part of the course by the fifth fairway. These were distinctly Bhutanese touches. But there was an equally familiar aura, too. Observing Tshering and his staff toil reminded me of the plight of golf course crews throughout the world—underpaid and overworked people sweating bullets day by day so that wealthy men can have emerald green manicured oases on which they whack little white balls into holes.

I looked at Tshering. His face was taught, tense, full of nervousness. He was the most stressed person I'd met since arriving, which was ironic. Golf courses are supposed to be tranquil getaways, but for many people they are the opposite. Golfers are often a jangle of nerves, fretting about their inability to play like a pro, while club staff are typically concerned about pleasing their highbrow bosses. I never expected to find this anxiety in Bhutan, but I did.

"I hope I can get everything done in time for the tournament," Tshering said. "The members want perfection."

I KNEW THE Bhutan Open was going to be, well, different from and infinitely more low-key than the U.S. Open. But this different? As I drove up to the Royal Thimphu clubhouse at seven-fifteen A.M., it was chilly and drizzling. The parking lot was empty except for a small huddle of people by the clubhouse. They were the cooks (all men) and waiters (all women), and they were sipping tea and rubbing their hands to stay warm. The course, too, was deserted. There were no big white corporate tents, no electronic scoreboards, no gallery ropes.

The practice tee also was dead. None of the other one hundred competitors were honing their swings, practicing their wedges, or grooving their rhythm. I suppose they were all asleep or having breakfast. Carrie had gone out to a couple of bars last night, and when she came home at about eleven, she told me that she'd seen many of the club members reveling.

By the first tee, Shayam, the starter, and Tshering, the super, were hanging a small banner on two bamboo poles. The banner said, 2002 BHUTAN OPEN.

There was, however, one sign of life. Benji was standing on the clubhouse steps, gazing out over the course. As I stood next to him, he began talking, but not to me. He continued looking out over the course. It was as if he were delivering a soliloquy. "I feel great," said Benji, his voice raspy but full of life. "A bit tired, because I was out all night and didn't sleep a wink, but maybe that'll play to my advantage."

As we stood there chatting, players began arriving, but they didn't resemble contenders for a national championship. Potbellied and middle-aged men with dirty golf shoes, spotted khakis, and argyle sweaters were dragging huge staff bags, the ones tour players use, on pull carts. Golf bags in the rest of the world have gotten dramatically smaller over the past decade, because people have finally begun to realize that having a 50-pound leather behemoth for a golf bag is not only impractical but also a big chore. But the opposite has happened in Bhutan, where bigger bags are the rage. The Bhutanese want to emulate professionals as much as possible, and the tour player bags are one way they can do that. Size doesn't matter in Bhutan, because everybody uses a pull cart.

The Bhutanese love gadgets, too. So hanging from the bags were steel-bristled groove-cleaning brushes and plastic tee-holders, things that no professional would be caught dead with on his bag. As for hitting practice balls, that was not a priority this morning for most players, either. "We don't practice before competitions," said I. J., a diminutive Indian Army officer. I. J. was wearing a small straw hat, the same kind that was Chi Chi Rodriguez's trademark. "Practice will make our handicaps too low, and then we won't get enough strokes in the tournament. But I would like to begin coaching with you after the tournament, okay?"

I WAS SHAKING when I reached the first tee at eight A.M. Never mind that most of the players in the field were everyday hackers playing with the same expectations as somebody buying a lottery ticket, and that only a few of the entrants could break 80. I was as nervous as I'd ever been in an amateur or college tournament.

My problem wasn't that since arriving in Bhutan I'd played only a few nine-hole rounds. No, I hadn't played in a real tournament in several years, so my mind was awash with uncertainty, which is a sure recipe for disaster in competitive golf. My three playing partners, however, were as calm as monks.

"Did you go out last night?" asked Dema, a short man whose teenage daughter attended my youth clinics.

"No. Having a baby doesn't leave much free time," I said.

"Don't you have a babysitter?" asked Pema Tshering, another member of our foursome. Pema's surprise that I had stayed home on a Friday night to take care of Claudia wasn't shocking. The Bhutanese men at Royal Thimphu, like golfers everywhere else, don't change many diapers.

My third partner was David Adair, a thirty-three-year-old Irishman with a thick brogue and a stocky rugby player's build. David was the boys' varsity soccer coach at Woodstock, a 150-year-old boarding school in Mussoorie, a hill station in the Himalayas in northeastern India. Many wealthy Bhutanese send their children to the plethora of boarding schools in northeastern India because they have much better academic standards than Bhutanese schools and the Indian schools offer athletics and other extracurricular activities, which are virtually nonexistent in the Bhutanese school system. Adair had brought his squad, which had a few Bhutanese players, to Bhutan for a series of matches against Bhutanese high school teams.

I'd met Adair three days ago when he and his team were having breakfast in the clubhouse at Royal Thimphu. He had been reticent after I suggested that he play in the Bhutan Open, claiming that he hadn't played much golf recently and that his handicap was 13. "That wouldn't qualify for my village championship in Ireland," he said. But after I explained that most of the

Bhutan Open participants would also be double-digit handicappers, Adair capitulated and paid the 500-ngultrum ($11) entry fee. Perhaps I should have kept my mouth shut.

Adair's tee shot on the first hole, the 100-yard downhill par 3, was a low screamer that zoomed left of the green into waist-high gorse. His caddie found the ball, but that was a mixed blessing. "This stuff is worse than what we have back home!" Adair yelled.

Adair took a few mad lashes to extricate his ball onto the green, and several putts later his ball, mercifully, plopped in the hole. I don't recall his score on the hole, but I don't think it was less than 10.

Things went downhill from there. Adair embarked on a series of of hooks, slices, worm burners, and whiffs that left Dema, Pema, and me in shock. Adair, amazingly, remained positively jolly. Yet after four holes he had lost several balls and taken a few dozen strokes, so it wasn't surprising when he announced, "I'm going to stop keeping score and play a friendly round with you all."

Nobody argued.

Adair continued playing horribly, but at least he was giving me something to be happy about. I, too, was playing horribly, but not *that* horribly, so I knew I'd beat at least one person. Still, Adair could take only so much suffering. After dribbling his drive into the marshy pond in front of the seventh tee, he was done. "I think I'll stop playing and walk the rest of the way," he said.

Again, nobody argued.

ADAIR WASN'T THE only player withering in the weeds. While walking along the second fairway, I gazed to the right at the rough that served as a buffer between the second and third fairways. An Indian Army officer whom I'd taught and recognized by face but not name was playing the third hole and looking for his ball with his caddie in the rough. Suddenly I saw the caddie kick something again and again. After several kicks, I saw a golf ball trickle into the third fairway. Then the Indian Army officer hit that ball up the third fairway.

I looked at Dema, who was a few yards from me, to gauge his reaction. He was unfazed, even though it was the most flagrant cheating I'd ever seen in a tournament.

"Did you see that?" I asked.

Dema shrugged his shoulders. "Those Indian Army guys, they always cheat," said Dema. "You have to look out for them."

I didn't know what to think or do. Dema had no intention of reporting the incident, and I definitely wasn't going to say anything as the new kid on the block.

The day's carnival atmosphere peaked when our group was waiting on the tee at the sixth hole, a flat, 180-yard par 3. Dema had just made an 8 at the fifth hole, but to my surprise he was happy. "That's very good for me," he said.

I was befuddled. "How can that be good?" I asked. "You're not such a bad golfer."

Dema smiled. "It's good because my handicap will go up. So please, keep giving me higher scores."

"Don't you want to play well? Don't you want to win?" I said.

Dema and Pema smiled, but I was just beginning to learn about the shady side of Bhutanese golfers, the same shady side that golfers everywhere seem to have. Dema wasn't just a happy-go-lucky Bhutanese unfazed by some bad shots. I now realized why I. J. had told me earlier in the day that he wanted to begin taking lessons *after* the tournament.

"High scores are good for the Maruti," Pema explained. "A higher handicap means a better chance to win the car."

This was my introduction to sandbagging in Bhutan. *Sandbagging* is a golf term for intentionally playing poorly to boost your handicap so when you play in tournaments with scoring based on handicaps, rather than gross scores, you'll have a better chance to win. Here's the logic: With an inflated handicap, you can play decently and your net score will be lower than it would have been had your handicap not been artificially high. In Dema's case, he was looking ahead to the crown jewel on the Bhutanese golf calendar—the India House tournament, a handicap-scoring event whose winner gets a new Maruti car.

In my mind, the Bhutan Open was the title to gun for. But the Bhutanese golfers didn't care about prestige. The pinnacle of golf for them was to win the car, and India House was just two weeks away.

STANDING IN THE fairway of the eighteenth hole of my first round, I looked at the sky. It was full of dark clouds that were dripping a light rain. I closed my weary eyes as drops dappled my face. I'd been playing golf for thirty-one years, since age four, but I'd never experienced such a maddening round. Finally I'd hit a straight drive and was laying one in the fairway. Then I envisioned something unusual: Guru Rinpoche flying on a tiger, his big, round face looking down at me with a grin.

I'm still not sure why I envisioned Rinpoche in the eighteenth fairway. I'm not Buddhist, and Rinpoche was not, by all accounts, a golfer. Perhaps, though, there's some truth to the stories that my Bhutanese friends have told me about Rinpoche and his proclivity to fly around on his tiger and heal people. Maybe on this afternoon, thirteen hundred years after Rinpoche's arrival in Bhutan, the revered lama had returned to sprinkle some of his positive karma on me. Heaven knows, I needed some.

I was eighteen over par and embarrassed. I had made a 10 on one hole and an 8 on another. I'd lost three balls, accrued nine penalty strokes, and fired my caddie on the eleventh hole. The little boy had been daydreaming for much of the round, and when he admitted that he hadn't watched my drive careen into the rough at eleven, I lost my temper and asked him to give me my bag. I paid him 100 ngultrums and carried my bag the rest of the way.

When Adair left us after nine holes, I'd felt like packing it in, too, but I'm not a quitter. Now with one more approach, crazy thoughts were swirling. Would the Royal Thimphu members lose faith in me as their pro? Was I qualified to teach a game at which I had been so inept? How could I have the nerve to tell people to play golf one shot at a time, with no regard for the past or the future, when I'd been unable to do that?

Then something funny happened. After lofting a crisp shot at the flag and two-putting for par, I signed my scorecard and gave it to Shayam, who was sitting in his little hut outside the club-house. The final tally: I'd shot 84, Dema 83, and Pema 103.

Shayam was one of my favorite employees at Royal Thim-phu. Charming and quiet, he had dropped out of school in his early teens and taken a job as a caddie to supplement his parents' income. Now in his midtwenties, Shayam was married and the doting father of a cherubic and well-mannered toddler son who often tagged along with his dad at the course. Shayam was seri-ous and polite when club members were around. He came from a much lower social and economic rung than they did, and he knew that most of the members demanded to be treated like masters of the universe. But during the many mornings we spent together as the lone people at Royal Thimphu, either playing some holes or with me giving him tips, Shayam loosened up. He enjoyed telling jokes and spinning yarns about the shenanigans at the club. One of his favorites was about the drunken old man who often passed out in the clubhouse and had to be carried to a car and driven home.

After Shayam transcribed my score into the tournament log, he looked up. "How many greens do you have on courses in America?" he asked.

"We have over twelve thousand courses," I replied.

"No, sir," Shayam gently said. "How many greens are there on a course?"

Shayam's query flummoxed me. Didn't he know that most courses have eighteen holes? More important, didn't he care why I'd played so badly? I kept waiting for Shayam to ask me about my awful day on the course, but he never did.

"Our courses have eighteen greens. That is the standard," I said.

Shayam smiled. "Wow, that is so many," he said. "Thank you, sir."

The Royal Thimphu members were similarly uninterested in how I'd played. Randy stopped me in front of the clubhouse to demonstrate a new way he'd held his hands when addressing the ball during the round. "How do my hands look?" he said, pretending to address a ball. His hands looked a little lower than they had in the past.

Before I could answer, Randy continued, "It feels great, and I played nicely." He had shot a three-over-par 69 and had a seven-shot lead over Lotey. Randy's success gave me a modicum of satisfaction; during our lesson this past week, I'd suggested that Randy lower his hands.

As the day passed, I realized how selfish and silly my concern over my score had been. No one cared but me. I was finally able to let go of my angst later that evening. I was upstairs in our bedroom at Benji's, typing on my laptop. Claudia was asleep in her portable crib against the wall, and Carrie had gone to dinner at a restaurant with some friends.

While typing, I heard the bedroom door creak open. I turned around from the desk and saw Kalpana at the door. She had a sweet, full smile, her red, dimpled cheeks full of joy. She was holding in her palms an apple pie she'd baked.

"For you, sir," said Kalpana.

Kalpana had no clue about the Bhutan Open or how I'd played. She was just a sweet woman who enjoyed cooking. I sat and ate the pie and forgot about my day at the Bhutan Open.

WINNING WASN'T IN the cards for me because of my poor play on Saturday. But Guru Rinpoche must have sprinkled some good karma on me the night before because things went much better on Sunday in my second round. I didn't have a whiff of nervousness and shot a respectable six-over 72 while playing with a captain from the Bhutanese Army and a twenty-two-year-old student. The student, Tashi Dorji Jr., was especially entertaining. Not because of his golf, which was atrocious, but because he was a bon vivant whose casual attitude and sarcastic wit reminded me of Rodney Dangerfield.

During the first few holes, Tashi Dorji played as poorly as Adair had played the day before, and Tashi Dorji's final score was well north of 100. But a day of tops, yips, and skulls didn't dampen Tashi Dorji's good-natured cheer and smile, both of which were beaming from the first tee to the eighteenth green.

Early on, Tashi repeatedly asked me for swing tips, but each time I politely declined. "This isn't the best place to take a lesson," I'd say.

Midway through the round, Tashi asked me how I met my wife. When I said that we had lived in the same dormitory during our freshman year at Cornell University, Tashi decided to give me his dating status at Garden City College in Bangalore, India, where he studied computer science. "I have lots of friends who are girls, but I don't like to get close," he said. "The girls will say, 'Come shopping with me' or 'Come over to my house.' But I like to be free and single."

"Will you ever get married?" I asked.

"I don't know," Tashi said. "But I like love, and I write poems about it. I have some poems on poetry.com. I write poems whenever I see love."

"Have you ever seen love on the golf course?" I replied.

"No way," Tashi said flatly. "Golf is fun, but it's a loveless game."

AFTER FINISHING MY second round at about noon, I returned to the course to watch the final group, which included Lotey and Randy, who were tied for first at twelve-over-par when I found them on the fifteenth hole. About thirty men were following the leaders on that cool, sunny afternoon. Leading up to the tournament, Randy and Lotey had been among the mellowest Bhutanese I'd met, which isn't surprising considering they're the two best golfers in Bhutan. They both speak and walk gently and deliberately, and the cadences of their golf swings are rhythmic and smooth.

At fifteen, Lotey took a one-shot lead when he drained a 15-foot putt for par and Randy made a bogey. Lotey gave a mighty Tiger Woods–like fist pump and yelled "Yes!" when his putt dropped, and I was surprised by the outburst. I could see that the veins in his neck and his face were much redder than normal, indicating that he was jacked up and nervous.

When the leaders reached the seventeenth tee, Lotey was ahead by two strokes. Randy hit the seventeenth green with his tee shot, while Lotey's ball sailed 10 yards over the green into a shallow swale. It was a precarious position. Lotey didn't have much green between the fringe and the flagstick; the green sloped away from him; and the wet turf was spongy, so there was a decent chance that Lotey would flub the shot.

I walked over to watch Lotey. With the gaggle of onlookers and me standing 20 feet away, Lotey lifted his ball with his hand because it had been plugged. Following the rules, he dropped the ball a few feet from its original position on much drier grass that was no closer to the hole than his original position.

I'll never forget what I saw next. Lotey stood behind his ball to line up the shot. Then as he walked toward the ball to go into the address position, he stopped just behind the ball and with one foot gently tamped down the grass directly behind the ball.

I was stunned. Lotey had cheated in plain view of his playing partners and the spectators. According to *The Rules of Golf*, "The ball must be played as it lies" and "A player must not improve or allow to be improved . . . the position or lie of his ball." Clearly, Lotey had stepped behind the ball to mush down the grass and give himself a better chance of making clean contact.

My heart was racing, but everybody else was nonchalant, as

if nothing had happened. But why? They, too, had seen Lotey improve his lie. I wondered whether the spectators knew the rules. Of course they did. Playing your ball as it lies is the game's most basic rule. Lotey also had to know the rule. He'd been playing the game for eons, was an excellent player, and had competed in international tournaments.

Lotey addressed his ball, swung, and made solid contact. The ball flew on a soft, low arc. It landed on the edge of the green, bounced a couple of times, rolled directly at the hole, clanked off the flagstick, and fell into the cup for a birdie. Lotey raised his arms in ecstasy. I shook my head in utter disbelief.

Cheating happens at every level of golf. How much it happens is hard to say, because evidence is largely anecdotal. At the 1985 Indonesian Open, Vijay Singh, then a fledgling pro, altered his scorecard to improve his score by one shot, and for that tour officials suspended him. A few years ago, the Starwood Hotels and Resorts company surveyed 410 business executives, and 82 percent of them admitted to cheating at golf.

Bhutanese golfers cheat, too. How much they cheat is impossible to say, but it's probably comparable to golfers in the rest of the world. Bhutanese have told me stories about cheating, mostly comical yarns involving guys cheerfully accusing their friends of rolling over balls to improve lies and taking gimmes on the greens. I've also heard more serious allegations. At the India House tournament a few years ago, the man who won the Maruti was accused by fellow competitors of recording doctored scores. Other players in the tournament suspected that this man had cheated and formally accused him.

The result was a heated debate among tournament officials about what to do. In the end, the accusers refused to testify to the tournament committee, so the cheating charges were dropped. "It was a very embarrassing situation, and we still don't know what really happened," a tournament official told me. Now I could see another ugly mess gathering right in front of me. Should I tell somebody about the cheating, or keep quiet and let the Bhutanese take care of their own tournament? If I didn't say anything and Lotey won, would I have a guilty conscience?

Now Randy stepped up to a 15-foot birdie putt that had taken on a sudden urgency. Missing the putt would have given Lotey a three-shot lead going to the final hole. Randy studied the putt from all angles and crouched down behind the ball to gauge the break. Alas, the putt rolled past the cup, and after making the short comebacker Randy's title hopes were all but quashed.

Next, Randy and Lotey walked side by side and in silence up the long, steep slope to the eighteenth tee. I watched them and wondered what was going through their heads. Was Lotey feeling guilty about having possibly cheated his way to the championship? Was Randy wondering what he should do about the cheating incident? Had Randy even noticed? I pondered these things as the spectators and I walked through fescue grass toward the eighteenth fairway. My heart was thumping, and I couldn't decide what to do. Finally I decided that I had to say something to somebody, so I approached Ugyen Dorji, aka Yougs, who was the tournament chairman.

"I saw it, Yougs," I said.

"So did I," he replied.

We were walking along the edge of the eighteenth fairway, almost parallel to where Lotey's and Randy's drives had landed.

"What are you going to do about it?" I asked.

"I'm not the marshal. I'll tell Tolly," said Yougs. He was referring to the golfer who had finished playing and was now working as a marshal for the final group. I liked Yougs's idea because Tolly, who was the chief of staff for His Majesty, was as fair and straightforward as anybody I'd met in Bhutan.

"Good," I said. "And don't let Lotey sign his scorecard until it's resolved."

If Lotey signed his card and was then determined to have cheated, he'd be disqualified. But if he didn't sign and was deemed to have cheated, he could add two strokes to his score, sign the card, and not be disqualified. While Yougs and I talked, several spectators eavesdropped, and the subject of our discussion spread in a flash. Soon everybody was whispering about whether Lotey had cheated. I was relieved. The guilt was no longer on my shoulders, and the Bhutanese would determine the ruling.

After the players hit their approaches, they and the spectators began walking toward the green.

Benji's brother Tobgye was now walking beside me. I asked him if he'd seen the cheating.

"Sure," Tobgye said. "Everybody was doing that today."

"Don't you guys play by the rules?" I said.

"We're getting much better at the rules," Tobgye said. "But it's not only the good players who do things. People can't seem to understand the concept of the ball in play."

As Tobgye spoke, we were approaching the green, and the spectators encircled the putting surface. Suddenly Lotey rushed toward me. Somebody had told him about my accusation, and he wasn't happy.

Lotey got to within 3 feet of me before Tobgye and a few

other men wrapped their arms around him and held him back. As they held Lotey, his face red with anger, he yelled, "If you accuse me, do it to my face!"

The suddenness and intensity of Lotey's aggression shocked me. I'd never seen anything like this in Bhutan, and his surge at me made me very afraid. Was I going to get punched? Hurt? Would we be on the next plane out of Bhutan? Perhaps my fear was severely overblown. The chances of Lotey punching me and of my family getting expelled from Bhutan might have been remote, if not nonexistent, but at the moment I felt like they were very real possibilities.

While the men continued restraining Lotey, he flailed his arms and continued screaming. "Accuse me to my face!" he kept saying.

After a couple of moments, Lotey calmed down, and the men convinced him to putt out. He grudgingly went back to the green.

Visibly shaking, Lotey three-putted for a double bogey. That gave Randy a chance to tie him for the title and force a sudden-death playoff. Randy had hit his short-iron approach weakly and it had landed in the small and shallow bunker to the front and right of the green, leaving him a relatively simple 15-yard shot. Holing it for a birdie would have erased Randy's three-shot deficit and sent the tournament into overtime. Randy hit a pure sand shot, nipping the ball cleanly, and it landed a few yards short of the flagstick and began trickling toward the hole. Alas, the ball stopped a few feet short. Randy missed the par putt and finished two shots back.

But all was not done. Randy hadn't necessarily lost. If the tournament committee decided to penalize Lotey for tamping down the grass behind his ball when chipping from near the seventeenth green, Lotey would be penalized two strokes, leaving him tied with Randy. Even worse, the committee could decide to disqualify Lotey.

The tournament committee huddled for a few minutes behind the eighteenth green. After they broke up their meeting, Yougs came over to tell me that they had determined that because most, if not all, of the players in the field had probably been improving their lies, no penalty would be given to Lotey. Yougs's explanation didn't make sense. Because others cheated, Lotey would be exonerated? But I was in no mood to argue.

While I was walking back to the clubhouse, a Bhutanese army brigadier who'd played in the tournament approached me and said, "Thanks for raising the issue. We have to put one severe rule into place."

About ten minutes after Lotey and Randy finished playing, there was a brief awards ceremony outside the clubhouse. While watching Lotey clench the trophy as the hundred or so spectators gave him warm and rousing applause, I decided that I needed to speak to Lotey. I wanted to explain how I felt, that I had no grudge toward him but was simply following the moral code of golf that impels observers to report potential rule breaches.

After the ceremony, Lotey walked toward the parking lot toting his clubs and the trophy. I scurried up from behind and asked if he'd sit and talk. I wasn't expecting Lotey to accept my invitation and I was half expecting him to scream at me or even try to hit me.

Instead, Lotey was calm and polite. "Sure, let's sit down and talk. I'm hungry," he said. "Can I get you something to eat, too?"

Minutes before, Lotey had tried to attack me, but now it was as if nothing had happened. I'd like to think that I could be so forgiving so quickly, but I'm not sure.

We sat down on the terrace surrounding the clubhouse. Lotey ordered hot tea and *ema datse*, a spicy dish, with white rice for both of us, and for the next thirty minutes he candidly told me about the cheating incident and his life.

Now forty-three, Lotey had grown up wanting to be a movie star, which was unusual in a country that at the time didn't have a film industry or a single actor. So at age twenty he took a bus to Bombay, checked into a cheap hotel, and spent the next several weeks wondering what to do. "I was so lonely, but I had my dream," said Lotey.

After about a month, Lotey bumped into a friend, Danny Denzongpa, a Sikkimese who was a fairly famous actor in Bollywood. "There is heavy competition, and you have no chance," Denzongpa told Lotey.

"That was very hard to take, but I didn't question it," said Lotey, who promptly got on a bus back to Bhutan.

Once home, Lotey became one of the most sought-after tour guides in his kingdom. He specialized in hard-core trekking, specifically the Snowman trek, a grueling month-long odyssey that skirts the Bhutan–Tibet border while crossing several high passes, including three above 16,000 feet.

After seven years of guiding, Lotey became a flight attendant with Druk Air, a job he held from 1987 to 2002. "I got scared after September eleventh and didn't want to fly anymore," said Lotey, who then became the general manager of a construction materials company.

Lotey's face was taut and smooth, like a marathon runner's, but he was a different man below the neck, with a modest potbelly. "I used to be so physically fit," he said.

"What happened?" I asked.

"The easy life is the lazy life," Lotey replied.

Over the past decade, Lotey supplemented his income through golf to help support his wife and three children (two boys and one girl). The prize for winning the Bhutan Open was a 21-inch Sony flat-screen TV worth about $600. "My wife doesn't like it when I play so much golf, but she likes what I bring home," Lotey said.

After speaking for twenty-five minutes, I was very confused. Lotey had been speaking calmly and without reservation, but it was as if nothing had happened. I wasn't sure whether I should keep talking and wait for him to raise the cheating incident, but finally I took the plunge. "What happened out at seventeen when you stepped behind your ball?" I said.

Lotey didn't blink or blush or have any reaction. He simply leaned forward and folded his arms on the table. "They call it a local rule, pushing down the grass. Now, since everybody is doing it in all the tournaments, our committee has not stood up on this," Lotey said. "We know it's not allowed [in the rules], but it's been how we do it."

"What do you do when you play outside Bhutan?" I asked.

"We can't do that," Lotey replied. "Outside, I never take a chance, because it's your name."

Lotey's reply didn't settle my mind. He admitted that he had cheated, but he didn't express an ounce of regret or admit to feeling an iota unsettled about having cheated. I wanted to press him further, but I didn't. I felt like a single question could cause Lotey to erupt, and I didn't want to cause another, and perhaps more serious, scene. I was a visitor, and there was nothing to be gained by pressing the case.

"It's kind of late, and I'm sure you want to get home," I said.

"Yes, that is good," Lotey said.

He rose from the table, slung his golf bag over his left shoulder, and began walking to the parking lot.

"What does being the Bhutan Open champion feel like?" I asked.

Lotey smiled. "This is an absolutely happy moment."

Chapter 9

HOUSEHUNTING IN OUR BACKYARD

STAYING OUT SO late most nights and having no job often conspired to keep Benji in bed until noon. But one Friday at eight A.M. in late September, Benji was chipper and lucid while having breakfast in the dining room with Carrie and me.

"What got you up so early?" said Carrie. "Must be a big date."

Benji chuckled. "I do have a date," he said. "But not with a woman. A consultant is visiting Bhutan and we're discussing carbon trading. It's nonexistent now, but it could become a big business here in Bhutan. I'm trying to get it going."

At first blush, carbon trading sounded like some crazy scheme, perhaps something a high-flying hedge fund would do. But as Benji explained the concept, his idea for a bona fide carbon trading venture in Bhutan seemed very realistic and potentially profitable. In a nutshell: Countries each have assigned amounts of carbon emissions they can generate from industry. If one nation produces less than its allotted amount, it can sell the unused amount of emissions, in the form of credits, to other nations or businesses. Bhutan has so little industry and its hydroelectric plants are so efficient that the kingdom has lots of credits to sell.

As a pioneer in environmental conservation, Benji was keenly aware of this situation and was seeking to make a profit for himself and the Bhutanese companies he would potentially represent.

As usual, KALPANA had prepared a breakfast feast for Carrie and me that included scrambled eggs, toast with butter and jelly, porridge, and orange juice. This wasn't the typical Bhutanese breakfast. Most Bhutanese, regardless of socioeconomic standing, eat the same thing for breakfast, lunch, and dinner: ema datse, which includes super-spicy chilies and melted cheese over a heaping pile of steamed rice. Some people throw cooked vegetables, such as broccoli, tomatoes, and green beans, onto their ema datse.

But Benji isn't a typical Bhutanese. Having spent so much of his time living outside the country, he developed a yen for an eclectic hodgepodge of cuisines. So this morning, Kalpana brought a tray into the dining room for Benji's breakfast that had a bizarre potpourri of food: some small slices of black fish imported from China, Tibetan rice balls, and steaming porridge and canned baby hot dogs from India.

"Yuck!" exclaimed Carrie when Benji took a bite of the fish.

"Silly American," Benji said with a laugh. "Take a bite and you'll think differently."

Carrie cringed. "No, thanks," she said.

Benji looked at me. I'm usually much more experimental with food than Carrie, the finickiest eater I know. For example, she eats tomatoes but not ketchup, and white rice in Bhutan but not white rice that I cook in New York. Still, I wasn't up to putting the squishy little fish, which smelled like sardines, into my mouth. "I'll pass, too," I said.

"Your loss," said Benji while chewing a bite of the fish.

"You must be sad that we're leaving you soon," said Carrie.

"You don't have to leave. You can stay here as long as you like," Benji said.

"We've already stayed too long," I said. "We want to get out of your hair."

It was early October. The few weeks we'd been in Benji's house had been exhilarating and without a moment of friction. Benji was always brimming with energy and bonhomie. When going out, he always offered to take us with him, whether it was to the grocery store, a snooker hall, or a dinner party; while at home he regaled us with stories so mind-jarring that just hearing them made the trip to Bhutan worthwhile.

Carrie and I often wondered whether Benji's stories were true. But Benji's friends would always confirm the veracity of something we'd heard, or Benji would offer evidence to prove himself. While describing his friendship with Sir Edmund Hillary, I wondered how Benji's and Hillary's paths could have crossed. Then Benji showed me a book written by Hillary that Hillary had autographed to him.

But Benji had never planned to host us for our entire stay. He had volunteered to house us for a few weeks, and although Benji never asked us to leave or in any way conveyed displeasure at us for remaining in his home, Carrie and I felt it was time to move out. We wanted to finally get our own place and live independently in Bhutan and tackle whatever challenges that would entail. The problem was that we couldn't find a place we liked. We visited one gorgeous modern two-level house, but it was twenty minutes outside of Thimphu. There was a brand new two-bedroom apartment that had bright pinewood walls and floors, but it was way up in Moithitang, the residential area high on a hill above the main commercial area of Thimphu and the golf course.

Finally, though, we found a perfect place. It was no surprise who found it for us—Benji, who suggested that we look at the house 100 yards down the hill from his. The home belonged to Tobgye Dorji, one of Benji's two older brothers. Benji told us that he'd lived in the house for a few years and so had his mother. The house was on the part of the hillside owned by Tobgye and sat just 75 yards from his home. When relatives weren't using it, Tobgye rented the house to expats, but it was now vacant.

At eight forty-five A.M. a car chugged into Benji's driveway and began honking. "We hear you, we hear you, Tobgye!" Benji yelled.

It was raining heavily, and the sky was ominously dark. A few days ago, it had been the Blessed Day of Rain, a Hindu holiday marking the last day of rainfall for the year, but the deities obviously weren't complying. (Hinduism is the second-biggest religion in Bhutan, most commonly practiced among the tens of thousands of Nepalese immigrants and the small but influential community of Indians in the kingdom.)

As Carrie and I scurried out of the house, Tobgye stuck his head out of the car window and bellowed, "Good morning!" His tone, strong but sweet, was just like Benji's. He also chuckled as he spoke, like Benji.

Tobgye was driving a Maruti 800, a four-passenger, four-door vehicle, but the smallest car I've ever been in and the most popular car in Bhutan. The Maruti, a product of India, is the modern-day Yugo, a dirt cheap yet surprisingly resilient vehicle.

The windows were totally fogged. "Should I turn on the defroster?" I asked.

"That would be nice," said Tobgye. "But there is no defroster."

"Is it broken?" I asked.

"No, it never existed," Tobgye replied.

Virtually no vehicles in Bhutan have defrosters; nor do they have heat or air-conditioning. The heat and AC aren't big deals, because the weather is rarely too hot or too cold. But having no defrosting blowers makes for situations both comical—with people driving with one hand on the steering wheel and another wiping the windows with a rag—and harrowing. It's impossible to keep the windows clear in many situations, so the Bhutanese often drive largely by instinct and with severely limited views of the road.

Tobgye's window was mostly fogged as he drove down the steep, rocky, and muddy road with his head hanging out of the car.

"I think you'll find the house is beautiful," Tobgye said as he pulled to the left and parked. There was a green picket fence with a small iron gate through which we walked. A stone path cut down through a little lawn to the back of the house, which was charming.

It was a green, one-level wooden ranch-style design with a triangular roof. It was surrounded by rose gardens, small swaths of grass interspersed amid slate walking paths. Best of all, though, was the view: a 180-degree panorama of the Thimphu Valley, with the dzong and golf course straight ahead, the downtown area to the left, and the less developed area dotted with farms, a military base, and some royal palaces to the right. Uphill and behind from the house was a forested hillside that climbed a few thousand feet to the ridge atop the valley wall.

I told Carrie, "This is it."

Inside, the house was simple and comfortable. It had a large master bedroom and a small second bedroom, a spacious living room, a modern (for Bhutan) kitchen, one full bathroom with a shower/bath, and a second smaller bathroom with just a toilet and sink. The house was very bright because every room had several windows. The furniture throughout was simple. In the living room, there were wood-framed chairs and sofas with cushions covered with Bhutanese textiles, and the windows had basic draperies in muted pink and green that looked like something you'd find at Target. The kitchen had a large steel sink and washing area, a wood dining table large enough to seat six, and a wall lined with cabinets and counters.

Just outside the kitchen, there was a one-room cement structure that housed some more kitchen appliances, including a full refrigerator, a small baking oven, and a counter with a cooking burner attached to a propane tank. Tobgye explained that this little structure was built to be the servants' quarters, but he'd turned it into an annex to the kitchen.

The best feature of the house was the porch attached to the extra kitchen. The porch was just a raised wooden platform covered by a wooden roof, but the view was anything but ordinary. It looked down to the Thimphu Valley, and at the middle of the panoramic view were the Thimphu dzong and the golf course.

"We'll be eating breakfast here every day," Carrie said.

I was beaming. "I could definitely get used to this," I said.

Carrie was holding Claudia. "What do you think, honey?" I said gazing into Claudia's blue eyes.

She smiled, but didn't say anything. No surprise. The girl was ten months old. Then she burped.

"Does that mean we should take it?" I said.

Claudia just kept smiling.

Carrie walked to the edge of the porch and turned to Claudia. "Do you want to make this our home?" Carrie said.

Claudia burped again.

"We'll take it," Carrie said.

"Very good," Tobgye said. "Come down to my house and have tea."

Tobgye led us along the stone path that leads through a small wooden gate set in a stone wall and down to his home. Suddenly three massive German shepherds stormed the gate while barking and jumping. I darted to the side. Carrie stepped back and yelled, "Whoa!" Tobgye was laughing.

"They wouldn't hurt a rabbit," Tobgye said. "Good thing nobody in Thimphu knows that. Otherwise I'd have to get real guard dogs."

Dogs are ubiquitous in Bhutan, from the bigger cities to the tiny mountain outposts. Most of the dogs are strays, and most of them are much smaller than German shepherds, but the mongrels are all unusually loud, especially at night. Many tourists complain about the canine concerts that alight on Thimphu, beginning at about ten or eleven P.M. and stretching usually until three or four in the morning. In the morning rush hour—well, "rush hour" is the term, not the mood, because nobody rushes in Bhutan—the streets and sidewalks are littered with sleeping dogs.

Carrie and I gingerly followed Tobgye through the gate and down the stone staircase to his house, where the German shepherds—Aysha, Keiser, and Bigfoot—hushed at his command and obediently followed us through the back door and into the kitchen.

We sat around a small round wooden dining table that looked like it had come from IKEA. The cramped dining area was stocked with stuff that reminded me of home—jelly; peanut butter; butter cookies; and best of all, a loaf of thickly sliced fresh bread.

"Where'd you get that?" I asked.

Tobgye pointed to the pass-through window through which was the cooking area. A bread-making machine sat on a counter.

"Any chance we can become regular customers for breakfast?" Carrie said.

"Our home is yours," said Tobgye.

Tobgye's personal history was as interesting as Benji's. After studying in India, Tobgye returned to Bhutan and began his career in 1969 as an officer in training in the Ministry of Trade and Industry. Quickly, though, Tobgye was given a new assignment by His Majesty: help start the Foreign Ministry. The king was amid the massive project of transforming the government from what had been basically the king and his confidants into a formal structure with divisions and a clear hierarchical structure. Tobgye's keen intelligence and affable demeanor made him perfect to represent Bhutan abroad.

Tobgye worked with a couple of other men to bring the Foreign Ministry to life. They cobbled together rules and bylaws by reviewing the way foreign ministries in other countries operated, and they had very little oversight in their day-to-day work. "It was loose, freewheeling, but very exciting, and we took our jobs very seriously," said Tobgye.

"That sounds a little like what Carrie is doing for your kingdom," I said.

Carrie's task of drafting a new evidence act and a new penal code for Bhutan was thrilling. While many of her lawyer peers were back in New York churning out billable hours at corporate law firms, Carrie was writing new laws for a country that was at a historical juncture similar to the 1770s in America. But Carrie was doing this kind of off-the-cuff. Unlike in Philadelphia back in the 1770s, Bhutan didn't have a sprawling group of legal geniuses bringing together its new laws. Yes, there was a large committee in Bhutan to draft the new constitution, but even much of that work was done by the chief justice himself.

So over the previous few weeks, Carrie had had a couple of meetings with the chief justice to map out her work. The chief justice assigned a High Court clerk and a secretary to help Carrie, who'd spent most of her time since arriving alone working on the penal code and evidence act. She'd been toiling out of a mostly unused one-floor office building about a half mile away from the High Court. She had a clean but spartan office with a wooden desk, a computer, a wooden chair, a sofa, and a single window.

"What's your work been like?" asked Tobgye.

"Daunting, but fun," said Carrie. "It's a huge honor but also a huge responsibility. It is hard trying to balance compassion, which is so essential to your people, and Buddhism, with justice."

While drafting the penal code and evidence act, Carrie was guided by the words of the chief justice. He had told Carrie that the Bhutanese legal system had been set up to give form and direction to the natural world and he instructed her with the following quotation from Benjamin Cardozo, the U.S. Supreme Court justice from the 1930s: "The final cause of law is the welfare of society."

Before starting to draft the new laws Carrie had given herself a quick tutorial in Bhutanese legal history. That basically consisted of studying two things. One was Shabdrung Namgyal, the Tibetan scholar-saint who unified Bhutan and codified its laws in the 1650s. In 1652, Shabdrung wrote a code of law that was based on Buddhism and included ten pious acts and sixteen virtuous acts. That code of law governed Bhutan for three centuries. The next upgrade in Bhutanese law came in 1959 when the National Assembly enacted the *Thrimzhung Chhenmo*, a comprehensive codified set of laws based on Shabdrung's code of law.

Next, Carrie had begun work on drafting Bhutan's new penal code and evidence act. She pored over similar legal documents from many other countries and used some American legal documents she'd packed in our luggage: the Federal Rules of Evidence, the Model Penal Code, and the New York Penal Code.

IN 1971, TOBGYE found himself getting sent abroad for diplomatic postings. His first assignment as a junior diplomat was in New Delhi, where he was until 1974, and then he was sent to New York as the deputy representative to the United Nations, from 1978 to 1984. After a year as ambassador to Bangladesh, Tobgye opened the Bhutanese mission to the United Nations in Geneva in 1985 and stayed until 1990. His final destination was Kuwait, where he remained until retiring and moving back to Bhutan in 1994.

Tobgye would likely have worked in more countries during his tenure with the Foreign Ministry, but Bhutan had diplomatic relations with only a dozen or so nations in the 1980s and '90s and today has them with twenty-two countries. There are several factors behind the paucity of formal global ties. One is money. Maintaining an embassy and supplying staff are costly, especially for a government that has an annual operating budget of $155 million, half of which comes from India. Also, Bhutan has long been fiercely protective of its national identity and wary of external influences, and establishing diplomatic relations usually involves a quid pro quo that is not always amenable. For example, Bhutan has no formal ties with the United States; if such ties were established, one Bhutanese government official told me, the United States might well want to station troops or CIA officers in Bhutan, which is in the center of a political hot spot. A Bhutanese diplomat speaking to the Associated Press in the late 1990s summed up Bhutan's wariness: "With diplomatic relations, foreign influences come in. [So] it's best for us to insulate ourselves from influence, at least formally."

Everywhere Tobgye went, he worked hard and had fun. Lots of fun. When I asked him what he liked best about New York, his face lit up like a kid on Christmas morning.

"Studio 54!" he said. He stood up and began mock disco dancing, gyrating his torso and waving his arms. This was hilarious: a Bhutanese man in a golf shirt and chinos doing a John Travolta imitation while eating homemade bread. "That place was *real* fun."

"You and Benji should have a talk show in Bhutan," I said. "You guys would be the best-watched program in the kingdom."

Tobgye laughed. "Yes, but then we'd get kicked off the air and thrown out of the country. We're too radical."

"So you could bring your act to America," I said. "We'd love you, too."

As we sat around the table and had tea, bread, and scrambled eggs, Tobgye took us on a peripatetic journey through his global travels. In New York, he never played golf. "I was too poor. The stipend barely gave me enough money to eat," he said. Geneva was no different, until he got lucky. "I hit the jackpot one night at a casino and the next morning I joined a country club."

Tobgye was Bhutan's ambassador to Kuwait for three years in the early 1990s, and as we ate, he went over to a cabinet in the dining area and removed a round plate of gold and silver. "The sheikh gave this to me as a gift," said Tobgye. "He used to invite us over for lunch. Wow! That man is huge. He eats like a horse!"

The more Carrie and I heard, the more we felt like our lives were terribly boring.

After we were done eating, Tobgye led us through his one-floor house. Around the corner from the kitchen and dining area was a formal dining room with a huge and fancy table covered with a white lace doily, similar to something you'd expect to find in a Park Avenue cooperative. That contrasted with the decidedly Bhutanese décor, including the Buddhist thangkas on the walls and the floor-to-ceiling prayer altar that was full of little Buddha statues, flowers, plastic necklaces, and other paraphernalia. Painted a rainbow of colors, the altar was kaleidoscopic. Most Bhutanese homes have an altar like Tobgye's, but most Bhutanese people do not pray as devotedly or as regularly as Tobgye, whom I often found prostrate and chanting Buddhist prayers in front of the altar.

The dining room leads to the living room, where virtually every wall, table, and inch of floor space was covered with Bhutanese artifacts—swords, helmets, bearskins, woven throne covers, painted thangkas, and pottery.

"It's like your National Museum in here," I remarked.

"No," said Tobgye. "It's the Pentagon."

"Huh?" Carrie said.

"Look around," Tobgye said. "There aren't any CIA agents, but there are five walls, just like your building in Washington. My wife and I designed this house without an architect. We did the outline of this room by laying a long piece of string along the ground. We tried to make it symmetrical, but it didn't work, which is why all the walls are a little different in length."

Suddenly Claudia, who was sleeping in her stroller in the living room, began crying.

"She's hungry," said Carrie. "She wants a bottle."

Fresh milk is not available in Bhutan, unless you live on a farm, and the pasteurized milk available in the disposable Tetra Paks and imported from India was potable but Carrie didn't trust it. So we lugged several cans of Kirkland-brand powdered baby formula from New York and mixed that with bottled water to make Claudia's bottles. Carrie had packed a baby bottle with formula and a bottle of water in the stroller, so I quickly added water to the baby bottle, mixed it, and fed Claudia.

"So has Claudia met any men yet in Bhutan?" Tobgye said, chuckling.

Carrie didn't return the smile.

"Not yet," I said. "But I'm hoping she meets Mr. Right and gets married."

Carrie still wasn't smiling. She looked at Claudia. "No, not you," Carrie said. "You're my baby and you're not meeting any men."

Chapter 10

DOES BIG BROTHER REALLY
CARE ABOUT *ME*?

THERE WAS A tan, 1970s-vintage plastic telephone sitting on a bamboo table in our living room, and it rang often. Usually the calls were for Carrie or our nanny/housekeeper; once in a while people called to say hello to Claudia, even though she could only babble. But on a placid October evening at eight-thirty P.M., the phone rang and Carrie got it. After talking for a minute, she held up her right index finger and bent it, signaling that the call was for me.

"It's Sonam Kesang," Carrie whispered. "He sounds kind of nervous."

Had I missed another date for a golf lesson? A few days earlier, I had neglected to write a lesson in my appointment book and blithely headed into town for lunch (tandoori chicken at the Hotel Tandori, which has the best Indian restaurant in the kingdom) while Randy waited in vain on the practice tee for a lesson.

"Rick, how are you?" said Sonam Kesang.

Sonam Kesang's voice was edgy and rushed. Something was awry.

"What are your plans tomorrow morning?" Sonam Kesang said.

"I've got a couple of lessons—" I said.

"We need to get together," Sonam Kesang interrupted.

"Sonam, Sonam," I replied. "What's going on?"

"We need to talk," Sonam Kesang said firmly. "The government is not happy with what you've written."

What? Carrie was lying on a couch reading, but when she saw my concerned look, she sat up. "What's going on?" she asked.

Immediately I knew what Sonam Kesang was talking about. Somebody—either a government official or an influential Bhutanese—had taken offense to an innocent quip about the king's wives that I had made at the beginning of a recent column I wrote on the *Sports Illustrated* Web site. Then the official called Sonam Kesang to have him relay the message to me, because he knew that Sonam Kesang was serving as our host during our stay.

Here's what I wrote:

> Ever wonder if Sasquatch is really a plus-3 handicap?
> How a king with four queens (all sisters) decides which
> three fill out his Saturday morning foursome?

I've long been aware of the strong Bhutanese sensitivity to public criticism and virtually any even remotely less than flattering comment about the royal family, so I'd been having Carrie edit my weekly columns. A few weeks earlier, Carrie had deleted a reference in one column to the crown prince dancing at a Thimphu nightclub while wearing a red leather jacket. "Why can't I mention that? Even the Bhutanese will be interested to know about their crown prince."

"Leave it in," Carrie tersely said, "and we'll be on the next plane out of the country."

Before I submitted my column with the quip about the king and his queens, Carrie had suggested that I delete the reference to the queens, but I didn't listen—and now I was perhaps in hot water.

I continued speaking to Sonam Kesang. "What did I say that was bad? I've only written nice things, tried to be fun and honest—"

Sonam Kesang was quick with his reply. "I'll meet you at the course at nine o'clock tomorrow. We'll go to my office and talk."

I hung up and stared through the window at the illuminated Thimphu dzong. My mind was racing. We'd just begun settling into the kingdom, feeling like we were residents and not visitors, and we absolutely loved being there. The warmth of the people, the fascinating Buddhist culture, the yak meat and sizzling chilies, my work teaching golf, Carrie's gig with the chief justice, Claudia's perpetual playdates with everybody she met, and the sense of freedom and independence she was gaining—we had so much to be grateful for.

Even dealing with problems had become fun. For example, it took a few weeks, and several visits and a few dozen phone calls to Bhutan Telecom, to get a dial-up Internet connection working on my laptop in our house. At first I was irate at the elliptical series of misinformation Bhutan Telecom representatives gave me. But I soon learned that things in Bhutan just don't happen as efficiently or immediately as they do in New York, and I'd come to appreciate and enjoy the much more relaxed and laid-back pace of activity in this kingdom.

BHUTAN HAS NO laws restricting freedom of the press, freedom of speech, and freedom of religion. There is nothing to prohibit public demonstrations. Indeed, Article 7 in the soon-to-be-enacted Bhutanese constitution promises "the right to freedom of speech, opinion and expression," "freedom of thought, conscience and religion" and "freedom of press, radio and television."

But the reality is that not everyone in Bhutan enjoys these freedoms. Just a few nights earlier, I went to dinner with a bunch of editors from *Kuensel*, a Bhutanese newspaper, and I heard several stories about how the government used to be a strong censor of the media in Bhutan. That's not surprising. *Kuensel* was founded in the late 1960s as an internal government bulletin and in 1986 it was transformed into a weekly newspaper. *Kuensel* became an autonomous corporation in 1992 and it no longer receives a government subsidy, but it remains partly owned by the government.

For the last two decades, no government officials have directly censored *Kuensel* or had any role in the editorial process, but the government's presence has always loomed large in the minds of the editors and writers. For them, criticizing and voicing blunt opinions is still not easy. "You don't fear punishment, but maybe you worry about what people will say," one editor told me. "Some people might even worry about their jobs."

Similarly, although it is legal to practice other religions besides Buddhism, it is illegal to build houses of worship that are not Buddhist or Hindu. As a result, Bhutanese Christians are forced to congregate in private homes. Many Christians complain that the government has even led minor campaigns to prevent Christian worship services in homes, although government officials deny this. Then there are examples of the Bhutanese restricting freedoms without any official provocation. For example, the Bhutan Broadcasting Service, a state-owned corporation and the only TV channel producing programming in Bhutan, has daily news telecasts, but they are more like announcements of major government activities and happenings in the kingdom, such as big traffic accidents and sports results. Criticism and debate are largely absent from BBS programs.

Public discourse, whether it's about the government or other institutions, also has been rare. The Bhutanese seem to have been generally quite satisfied with their kingdom, its government, and especially the king, and the absence of politics created an atmosphere that was mostly devoid of public criticism. But a relatively passive and quiet public is not to be unexpected. Remember, Bhutan is still a monarchy and less than fifty years removed from feudalism.

NOT LONG AFTER speaking to Sonam Kesang, I called some Bhutanese friends, hoping to find out exactly what was happening. The first person I called was a friend from Royal Thimphu who was a retired civil servant; he was shocked to hear that somebody had taken such offense to my column that the Foreign Ministry contacted Sonam Kesang.

"Why would anybody react like *that* to your article?" he said. "This is supposed to be a democracy, no? I don't think you need to do anything, and this will all go away."

My friend's suggestion didn't placate my fears. Perhaps I was overreacting? Maybe Sonam Kesang also went overboard? It's possible that somebody from the Foreign Ministry called Sonam Kesang and asked simply that I be careful with what I write but that everything was okay. Even if that was the case and the intentions were benign, it would still be very unsettling. It was unnerving to think that I was in a foreign country as remote as Bhutan and government officials were reading what I wrote and reacting to it by sending me a message.

So I persisted in my quest to find out what had transpired and what I could do. Next I called a friend who had a contact in the Foreign Ministry. He was not too surprised, but he offered to call his friend to get some inside information. A few minutes later he called me back. "No big deal," my friend said. "Relax, buddy. Everything's okay. My friend says it's no big deal."

No big deal? Then why did my friend tell me that, according to his contact, "people" in the Foreign Ministry did, in fact, read my story and take offense to my joke about the queens and suggest to Sonam Kesang that I avoid making references to the royal family? To me, it seemed serious to know that the government was reading what I wrote.

THE FOLLOWING MORNING I gave a lesson at eight A.M. and then went to the clubhouse for my usual breakfast—two eggs over easy, toast with butter, pork fried rice, and orange juice—and waited for Sonam Kesang. By nine-thirty he hadn't showed up, and wild thoughts begin racing through my head. Did Sonam Kesang get called into the Foreign Ministry for a special meeting about my column? Was the government so offended that they expelled my family and me, and now Sonam Kesang was arranging for our immediate departure?

Again, I might have been overreacting, but it was impossible to contain my fears. I sat inside the clubhouse until ten-thirty, when a waitress told me I had a phone call. It was Sonam Kesang.

"I can't meet today," said Sonam Kesang. "How about tomorrow morning?"

Sonam Kesang's voice was relaxed, nonchalant.

"Is everything okay?" I asked.

"I spoke to some people and nothing is going to happen," Sonam Kesang said. "It'll all be okay."

Sonam Kesang hung up. I was a bit calmer, but still my nerves were jangled. How could things change so fast?

I called my friend with the contact in the Foreign Ministry. The contact was happy to meet me at the Foreign Ministry and tell me what had happened, and thirty minutes later I was at the Foreign Ministry, on the second floor of the National Assembly building in Thimphu.

The building was big and imposing, like the Thimphu dzong, with sprawling corridors and towering ceilings and the offices were so quiet I wondered if anybody worked there. I passed by the entrance to the cavernous hall where the National Assembly meets. The space looked a little like the General Assembly meeting hall at the United Nations, with a stage up front and semicircular rows of seats for the 150 National Assembly members. (In 2006 there were 146 men and 4 women.) There was one main difference from the United Nations hall, however: The National Assembly hall had decidedly Bhutanese décor with Buddhist motifs painted and handcarved all over the ceiling and walls.

My friend's contact was a communications officer who worked at a desk in an open area with a few others. I was shaking from nerves, but the contact was as calm as a lama. Smiling, too.

"Everything is fine, don't worry at all," the contact said.

"If it's fine, then why did Sonam Kesang get a call last night?" I asked nervously.

"Somebody called him, but there's no problem."

"Do people in your office really read stuff that's written about Bhutan?" I asked.

"Sure, but we're just trying to be aware of what people say about us. There's no harm intended."

"Who read my columns," I asked.

"I'm not exactly sure."

"Then how do you know somebody read them?" I asked.

"I've been told that," the contact said. "Please, Rick. You can be sure that everything is just fine. Many people actually enjoy what you write. It is quite funny sometimes."

Rather than press the issue, I decided it was best to let it go. Whatever happened, somebody in the Foreign Ministry must have decided that I'd gotten the point—tone down my rhetoric about the royal family—and that nothing more needed to be done. I thanked the contact and said I had some lessons scheduled at Royal Thimphu that afternoon.

While walking the mile back to the course, winding along the Thimphu River, over a small two-lane concrete bridge, and then up a big hill, I tried to make sense of the bizarre events. But I couldn't.

THE FOLLOWING MORNING, after another restless night, Sonam Kesang picked me up at our house and drove me to his office, a small single-level dwelling that he had converted into his tour company headquarters. One room housed his office, and another room was used to store trekking gear for his groups and old golf equipment. I asked Sonam Kesang about the Foreign Ministry and who started this whole affair, but he was evasive, pretending he didn't hear me. Instead of answering my question, he pointed to a tall gray steel cabinet.

"Guess what's inside," said Sonam Kesang.

"Sasquatch," I said.

Sonam Kesang laughed. "One more guess," he said.

"Guru Rinpoche," I said.

Sonam Kesang chuckled again, and then he rose from his swivelling black leather desk chair and walked to the armoire. As he swung open one of the two doors, my eyes widened. The shelves were stocked with golf gear—balls, tees, shoes, gloves, grips, shirts, divot repair tools, caps, and more—and it was all in unopened packages. "This is the only pro shop in the kingdom," Sonam Kesang said proudly. "I make hardly any money, because I have to buy everything at retail from stores in Bangkok, but it's a fun little operation."

Finally I asked Sonam Kesang again: What's going on with the Foreign Ministry? But he only vented about how his government operates, which is probably not too different from how the U.S. government operates.

"Officials in our government have to make themselves useful," Sonam Kesang said. "So they do silly stuff and make issues out of nothing just to make noise. The civil servants have to pretend they're doing work."

"They sure made a lot of noise about me," I said.

Sitting behind his wooden desk, Sonam Kesang was wearing a red golf shirt, khaki pants, and a black Titleist golf cap. "That's life in Bhutan, and there's nothing else we can do about it," he said. "Let's forget the whole thing. I want to go play golf."

Case closed, I guess. If Sonam Kesang was okay then I was okay. He was a Bhutanese with a vast network of connections, and he was a good friend, so I didn't think he'd let me believe I was not in trouble if, in fact, I was. So I was at least okay enough to stop worrying that I might get called into the Foreign Ministry to explain myself and be booted out of Bhutan.

What did I learn from the experience?

I learned that you don't have to physically censor somebody to make them stop writing something. For the rest of my stay, whenever I sat at my computer writing, I always felt like somebody was looking over my shoulder, and I definitely toned down the rhetoric in my columns and made sure to avoid quips and criticisms about the royal family.

I also learned how many friends I had made in Bhutan. On the night Sonam Kesang called, I had several Bhutanese to call for advice on how to handle the situation. It was very comforting to have so many local people I knew well enough to call in that delicate situation, and it was even more heartening that everybody offered to help resolve the situation.

But the biggest lesson might have involved Carrie. While sitting in Sonam Kesang's Land Cruiser as he drove me to the course, I couldn't stop thinking about the warning Carrie had given me after she read the line about the king and his four queens. Had I heeded Carrie's advice, none of this would have happened. It had taken seven years of marriage, and eight years of dating before that, but I think I'd finally learned a very important lesson: Women know best, and men should put aside their egos and listen.

Chapter 11

HELLO, LINDA, WE'RE GOING
TO A WEDDING

STOCKY LIKE A linebacker, deeply tan like most Bhutanese, and gray-haired with a quarter-inch crew cut, Dasho Pem L. Dorji swaggered up to the practice tee at Royal Thimphu. While I tried to go on teaching my lesson, Dorji, wearing a colorful gho, knee-high argyle socks, and black loafers, waltzed along the range, glad-handing everybody like a politician. I knew a few things about Dorji from my trusty Lonely Planet guidebook: Since 1997 he had been the *dzongdag*, or governor, of Wangdi, the largest of the kingdom's twenty districts, and for five years before 1997 he was the dzongdag of the Bumthang district. The guidebook, I remembered, also mentioned that he was "strict about cleanliness." When I read it, I was picturing a button-down tough guy—a Bhutanese Rudy Giuliani, not a Bhutanese Dean Martin.

Standing next to the man I was teaching, Dorji grabbed a driver out of a friend's bag and began blasting balls. He hit a little blooping fade that one of the caddies shagging balls out in the fairway caught with his bare hands. He hit a snap hook that whistled no more that 10 feet off the ground for a little while and then vroomed down into some thick fescue. Then he hit a low line drive that whistled down the middle of the fairway and narrowly missed the head of a caddie who wasn't watching. After each lunge, Dorji's short, jerky swing sent him way off balance so he'd wobble on his heels and almost tip over backward.

"How's this look, Rick?" Dorji asked, with the air of a man expecting a compliment. He hit another bloop fade.

"Sir, your action looks pretty good," I said. I was lying, of course. Dorji's swing was awful. But I wouldn't tell Rudy Giuliani his swing stunk, either.

"Don't call me, 'sir,'" Dorji said in a gravelly voice. "I'm Habu."

"Yes, sir. . . . I mean Habu," I said. "But why Habu?"

"That's what everybody calls me," he said. "It's some silly nickname I got in school."

"What's the name mean?" I asked.

Habu shrugged his shoulders. "Nothing," he said. "Just one of those names your friends give you for some reason that you never remember."

"Your action could use some help," I said. "But I'm very impressed that you can swing wearing a gho. I've never seen anybody do that."

Habu looked up from his intense ball-beating session and looked me in the eye with an impish grin. "Maybe *that's* my problem." he said. "His Majesty is the only man who can play this game in a gho."

After whapping a few more balls, Habu put the driver back into a bag—it was the wrong bag, but instead of saying anything, I quietly moved the club back to the correct bag—and then turned to talk to me. He said, "Rick, you and your wife will be my guests at my daughter's wedding next weekend. And I want you to bring that adorable baby girl. I want to meet her."

This was the first time I'd met Habu. How did he know so much about my family and me? Why did he invite me—or rather, command me—to come to a wedding? Had my burgeoning fame in this little kingdom preceded me? Maybe I could move here and open a teaching academy and become the Butch Harmon of Bhutan? It sure was amazing how much of a good reputation you can build among a bunch of movers and shakers simply by teaching them how to correctly hit a golf ball.

"We'd love to come, but there's a problem," I said. "In a few days, my mother-in-law is coming to Bhutan from New York—"

Habu interrupted me. "She'll be my guest, too. We'll see you on Friday night."

Habu twirled around and jogged up the hill to the parking lot. He hopped in the front passenger seat of a white Land Cruiser, and the vehicle drove away. Back on the practice tee, Yougs took a break from hitting balls to tell me about Habu. "Some people love him, some people hate him," said Yougs. "He governs with an iron fist, but he gets the job done. He turned Wangdi from a pigsty into the cleanest place in our country. Habu wants things done yesterday, and he wants them done right. If people don't listen, they pay the price."

"What price?" I asked.

"Maybe a fine, or he might slap somebody with a stick like a schoolteacher," said Yougs.

The town of Wangdi, the largest and only legitimate town in the Wangdi district, is home to the district's top government offices, including the district dzong, where Habu works. But Wangdi is hardly populous. Physically it's big, comprising much more land than the other nineteen districts in the kingdom, but the whole district has only thirty-two thousand people, a number exceeded by eight other districts. The town itself and its environs stretch for dozens of square miles, but the town center is just a dusty little space about half the size of the Great Lawn in Central Park. I knew because we visited Wangdi while touring Bhutan in 2000, so I could picture Habu stomping around the town center and yelling at shopkeepers to sweep the streets and sidewalks and clean their one-floor wooden shops. I also recalled that the town was full of big black plastic garbage cans with yellow USE ME signs painted on the sides. "Habu put those cans all over Bumthang," Yougs told me. "People thought he was crazy, but having them helped clean up that place so he put them in Wangdi."

After my lesson, at about four P.M. I walked into downtown Thimphu and found an Internet café. Two years ago, I didn't see any Internet cafés in Thimphu, but now there were half a dozen. The one I visited was called Cyber Café. It was clean and simple—a single room on the second floor of a small four-floor office-building-cum-mall that also included a pharmacy, a photocopy shop, a bar with snooker tables, and some offices. Just inside Cyber Café's entrance was a little desk where a man wearing blue jeans and a gray button-down oxford shirt and a woman wearing a kira—each of them appeared to be about twenty-five—were sitting and talking.

Once I booted up my e-mail server, I sent a message to Linda, my mother-in-law. She was coming to visit for three weeks, and I was excited to tell her about our plans to attend the wedding. In the e-mail, I proposed an itinerary: First, she'd spend a few days in Thimphu. Then she'd attend the wedding in Wangdi with us. After that, I'd remain in Thimphu to teach golf while

Linda, Carrie, and Claudia made a ten-day journey to the Bumthang district in central Bhutan, a cultural treasure trove of historic monasteries, temples, and palaces, amid four parallel mountain valleys that are renowned for their natural beauty.

The next day, Linda replied by saying that she, too, was excited. She had just one question: "What do you wear to a Bhutanese wedding?"

THE BETTER QUESTION, as it turned out, might have been, "Can you rent a helicopter so I don't have to drive across Bhutan?"

The answer would have been "No," but not because of the cost. There are no helicopters in Bhutan.

Linda survived the vertiginous descent into the Paro airport just fine, and she napped through the harrowing, cliffside drive to Thimphu. But just forty-five minutes into the drive to Wangdi, her eyes were half closed, her face was pale, and her head was listing. We were bumping along in a rented Land Cruiser with a driver named Sonam (Bhutanese who rent cars to foreigners usually also provide a driver), traversing a narrow, twisty, terrifying road through the Thimphu foothills. Every few miles there was one of those diamond-shaped yellow road signs with a black zigzag, intended to warn drivers of upcoming switchbacks, but the signs seemed superfluous. This route, like all Bhutanese roads, was a series of nonstop switchbacks, clinging by their toenails to cliffs that drop into bottomless, densely wooded, car-hungry chasms.

After a month in the kingdom, Carrie, Claudia, and I were relaxed and getting used to driving in Bhutan, but this was Linda's first long trip. It looked as if it would be a memorable one.

We were climbing uphill toward Dochu La, an 11,000-foot-high pass, 15 miles west of Thimphu. From the top of the pass on a clear day, there's an unobstructed panoramic view of the snow-capped peaks that run along the border between northern Bhutan and southern Tibet. Sonam slipped a cassette into the stereo, and "We Will Rock You" started pumping out of the speakers. In the passenger seat, Linda looked, for lack of a better word, rocked. No blood in her face. Big disgrace. Prepared, once she got her strength back, to start kicking my tail all over the place. Then Queen stopped, and Diana Ross started. It's "Ain't No Mountain High Enough," and I thought I heard Linda moan in quiet but heartfelt dissent. I prayed that the gorgeous view from the top would make amends for the rough ride.

But as we approached the summit, we entered a soupy fog so thick I could barely see a few feet ahead. Strange. Just a minute before, there had been a bright blue sky. Sonam pulled over to the side of the road, parking at the base of a driveway that led up to a café and observatory popular with tourists. We all got out of the SUV and stood in the crisp morning chill.

"Major bummer," I said. "The mountains are right there." I pointed in the direction of the peaks, wishing we could see them. "They're amazing because they look so peaceful."

Despite the fog, it was not a total loss. We could see the hundreds of colorful prayer flags fluttering on tall wooden poles that sit atop the pass, and the kaleidoscope of colors and the flapping noise of the flags were enough to give us goose bumps.

"Maybe we'll get lucky and see the peaks on the way back," I said.

Linda gamely managed a faint smile. "Okay, maybe next time," she said weakly as we got back into the Land Cruiser.

The remaining ninety minutes of the drive were blessedly

mellow. We had to traverse another fifteen minutes of switch-backs, but the fog mercifully prevented Linda from seeing over the cliffs. Then the road became gentler and the sharp switch-backs settled into smaller curves. The final twenty minutes took us through little farming villages dotted with terraced rice pad-dies and wheat and potato fields. Goats and cows languidly munched grass and shrubs by the roadside. The pastoral setting seemed to revive Linda, a professional photographer back home on Long Island, who now was taking pictures while leaning out the window.

It was six P.M. when we arrived at our hotel, the Y.T. Lodge, a modest two-floor, twenty-room concrete structure painted white. We were in Lobesa, a village 6 miles west of Wangdi, with stunning views of the wide, sinewy Wangdi River and of the val-leys that snake through the region. The rectangular lodge had green shutters on the windows and resembled a motel you'd find on a country road in upstate New York, with one exception: Lush gardens teemed with brilliant mountain flowers, banana trees, and huge bougainvillea bushes with red and pink blooms.

While we unloaded the luggage and stretched in the little as-phalt parking lot, a short and portly man with a cheerful, round face, a scraggly goatee, and wispy black hair greeted us. "You are my guests," he said. "The governor and I have been friends since boyhood."

I assumed that this charming man was Y.T., the lodge owner whom Habu had told me about when he suggested we stay here. Y.T. bent forward at the waist, stretched forth his arms, and turned the palms of both hands skyward. "It is my pleasure to have you, friends," Y.T. said in clipped English. "Please, make yourselves at home. We will drive up to the dzong for dinner."

Y.T. was referring to the Wangdi dzong, one of the most

impressive and imposing dzongs in Bhutan. The dzong was built nearly four centuries ago at the request of Shabdrung Namgyal, the man who unified several disparate fiefdoms into the kingdom of Bhutan, and it sits in a dramatic position at the tip of a peninsula, 200 feet above the confluence of two wide and roaring rivers. Habu lived in the Wangdi governor's house, near the dzong entrance, and the wedding party was to officially begin that night with a dinner in the grass courtyard between Habu's home and the dzong's entrance.

Y.T. led us to our rooms. First we came to the room for Carrie, Claudia, and me. It was 12 feet long and 10 feet wide, with white walls. The ceiling had several thick wooden beams, each a few feet apart, and the beams were covered with painted lotus flowers, a popular Buddhist symbol, while the drapes had painted scenes of a Bhutanese folktale involving dragons, lions, and monks.

I set up the portable crib for Claudia and put her inside with a few toys. While she drifted off, I changed into a blue oxford shirt with a red tie and khaki pants. Meanwhile, Carrie had dresses, sweaters, pants, shoes, scarves, and a Bhutanese kira strewn across the room. She was putting on and taking off clothes a mile a minute.

"What am I going to wear?" Carrie muttered. "I have nothing!"

Linda knocked on our door, which was ajar, and came inside. "Are you ready?" she asked.

"Mom, I can't go because nothing works!" Carrie exclaimed.

Linda, who was wearing a flowery one-piece dress with a shawl, laughed. She said, "When I told my friends I'd be going to a wedding in Bhutan, the first thing everybody asked was, 'What will you wear?' That was bizarre. Nobody cared whose wedding it was or what the ceremony would be like."

Carrie, too, had clothes on her mind. Indeed, she was oblivious to everything around her while immersed in a desperate search for the perfect outfit. She was a slowly gathering tornado, clothes flying as she whirled in circles, changing from one outfit to another. After ten minutes the storm calmed and Carrie stood still. She looked at Linda, Claudia, and me, quietly sitting on a bed next to each other. Carrie was wearing a lavender-pink silk kira jacket, black slacks, and black strapped heels. She looked great.

"Come on," said Carrie, marching toward the hallway. "We're late."

"Forgetting something?" I said.

Carrie was in the hallway. "What now?" she said.

"Your daughter is still in her crib," I said.

AFTER A FIFTEEN-MINUTE drive that took us along the Wangdi River, over a 150-yard-long steel and concrete arch bridge, and finally up a very steep hill, we were in Wangdi. The center of the dusty commercial area was a blacktopped parking lot with two gasoline pumps in the middle of it, and surrounding the lot were rickety, one-floor wooden shops, one next to another, that reminded me of New York bodegas because they all sold a little bit of everything, from bottled water to hot pots to rice cookers to wool blankets to flip-flops to whiskey.

I was trying to imagine what the wedding would be like, but I had no clue. The Bhutanese I'd asked had only told me that it would be fun and that the food would be good. My guess was that the wedding would be a sedate affair punctuated by Buddhist rituals and recitations and perhaps officiated by monks.

We passed through the village and turned right through a big arch, then drove a quarter mile to the Wangdi dzong and Habu's house. The driveway was festooned with candles, brightly colored prayer flags, and white banners with colorful dragons, lotus flowers, and other Buddhist symbols. Habu's house was also adorned with Buddhist décor, the most impressive item being the rice mandala on the front walkway. The mandala was the size of two beach towels sitting side by side, and uncooked rice grains painted red, green, blue, yellow, and black had been used to create a collection of Buddhist symbols, including a dharma wheel and lotus flowers. Monks trained in the arts are hired to create such works for the most special occasions in Bhutan, and this spectacular mandala took days to complete.

As we disembarked from the Land Cruiser, Habu shuffled up to us, holding a glass of whiskey. "Linda, baby, welcome to Bhutan," he exclaimed.

Habu gently wrapped his arms around Linda, then sidled over to me. I was holding Claudia, and he stuck his face right in front of hers. "Oh, my little darling, I am so honored to meet you," Habu said gently. "You will have fun."

The driveway was full of people, most of them wearing ghos and kiras, although a few men were in business suits. Some of the guests were sitting in the lawn chairs scattered about the driveway; others were milling around, chatting; and some were dancing to the rock music blaring from a boom box. Following Buddhist tradition, the wedding ceremony had taken place earlier that morning in a private service that was presided over by a monk in a prayer room in Habu's home; only a few family members and close friends had been on hand, although other people could have attended.

"I wish you'd told me," I said. "I would've liked to have seen the ceremony."

"It was so long," said Habu. "Next time. But it was very beautiful."

Meanwhile, about 30 yards away, on a lawn by a cliff that drops down to one of the rivers, there was a relaxed form of entertainment: A dozen women in kiras and black high heels were performing traditional Bhutanese dances, most of which involved the women dancing in circles or in two parallel lines and chanting folk songs. To the Bhutanese, I thought, this dancing must be boring, because none of the native guests were paying attention to their native dance troupe. I, however, was entranced. The dancing had a mesmerizing rhythm that lulled me into a kind of foggy trance.

But nearby, in the driveway, the party was jumping.

"Linda, baby, can I get you a drink?" Habu said, beaming a smile as big as a prayer wheel. Habu gave a hand signal to a woman who appeared to be a servant. "Hey, over here. Show my special guests to their seats," said Habu. The woman ushered us to lawn chairs right next to those reserved for Habu's family.

We'd been in Wangdi for only a few hours, but I sensed that Linda was exceedingly happy. I think she liked the royal treatment, getting greeted as special guests everyplace we went. "This really is a happy place," Linda said.

Habu played court jester all night and gaily introduced us to everybody. The first person we met was his older brother, Benjor. "He used to be governor here in Wangdi," Habu bellowed. "Now he's a businessman. Smart guy, isn't he, getting out of politics?"

Benjor was the biggest Bhutanese I'd met: 6'1" and 200 pounds, with a voice deep and raspy, perhaps from smoking.

"Was your wedding like this?" I asked Benjor.

He smiles. "Oh, no, it was quieter," he said. "We were married so long ago, when life was quieter."

"When?" I asked.

"Nineteen seventy-six. Neil Armstrong attended the wedding," he said.

"The astronaut?" Linda asked in disbelief.

"Of course," Benjor said. "He was in Bhutan on a goodwill tour with pictures and a slide projector. He even donated a rock from the moon to our National Museum in Paro."

Benjor looked up to the full moon and continued, "At one dinner gathering, Mr. Armstrong told a group of elderly people, including my father, about walking on the moon. Nobody believed him. One man said, 'Yeah, and I walked across the water.' My father knew about the moon walk, though, so he tried to tell his friends that Mr. Armstrong was telling the truth. At one point Mr. Armstrong pointed up to the moon and said, 'That's where I was.' Another old man replied, 'C'mon, you've had too much wine tonight.'"

With his gift for gab and reservoir of A-list celebrity stories, Benjor was a sedate version of Benji. One of Benjor's favorite stories involved a visit Demi Moore made to Bhutan while Benjor was the governor of Wangdi. When Moore traveled through Wangdi, she stopped at one of the little shops to get some snacks and saw a poster of herself on the shop wall. She told the shopkeeper that she was the woman in the poster, but the shopkeeper was unmoved and said, "Yeah, right. Please just pay me."

Throughout the rest of the night, the crowd of fifty guests ate, drank, danced, and talked until midnight under a clear sky illumined by more stars than I'd ever seen. The Bhutanese treated us like family, especially Claudia, who spent the night being passed from person to person.

At about ten P.M. we decided to head back to Y.T.'s. Claudia had been sleeping in her stroller for a while, and Carrie, Linda, and I wanted to get some rest for what Habu had told us would be a long and festive second day. "The party starts in the late morning and it'll go until, well, who knows?" he said.

I'm not sure the king had weddings in mind when he conjured up gross national happiness, but the phrase aptly describes the mood at Habu's house.

BACK AT Y.T.'S, Carrie and Linda took Claudia inside while I lingered in the parking lot. I spoke with a Bhutanese man who had also gone to the wedding. The man was a banker, and his face glowed when I asked if he'd ever been to America. "I studied at Auburn. Go, Tigers!" he said while pumping his fist as if cheering at a football game.

This was bizarre. I was in a remote part of one of the planet's most remote countries, listening to a native tell me about his rabid passion for SEC football and his graduate studies in Alabama. What next? Would he tell me that he rode in a bus with Rosa Parks?

"I spent two Christmases in New York and loved it," he continued. "I drove to New York alone from Alabama, through Louisiana and Mississippi and New Hampshire."

"But New Hampshire is way north of New York," I said. "You must have been very lost."

"No, I just wanted to see New Hampshire," he replied nonchalantly.

The man said good night, but I remained in the parking lot, gazing into the night. I started to laugh, spirited by an image in my mind. I pictured an Auburn football game. Jordan-Hare Stadium is rocking with eighty-five thousand rabid spectators. Auburn's cheerleaders are making a pyramid, the young men and women leaping and being raised higher and higher. The pyramid is complete except for the final person on top. Next, a Bhutanese man, wearing a gho, dashes down to the field from the stands, runs up to the pyramid, and the cheerleaders loft him up to the top. The man raises his arms to the sky and yells, "Go Tigers go!"

Chapter 12

THE WEDDING CONTINUES, WITH LAMAS, POODLES, AND YUMMY HORNETS

ADVICE TO ANYBODY attending his first Bhutanese wedding: Bring sunblock.

Back in Thimphu, somebody had told Carrie that Saturday's festivities would include lots of dancing and eating and all of it would happen outside, so thankfully, my brilliant wife properly planned for day two of the wedding and brought a tube of SPF 45. Of course, the same sun shines on both Bhutan and New York, but the rays feel much stronger in Bhutan because you're a lot closer to the sun.

More advice to anybody attending his first Bhutanese wedding: Don't eat the week before.

The first night's buffet was overwhelming, but it seemed like an appetizer compared to the Romanesque spread on the second day.

Day two began when Sonam drove us down Habu's driveway at ten o'clock and dropped us in front of a rectangular white tent that was open to the sky in the middle and had a roof covering only the seating areas on the sides. There were three rows of folding chairs along each side of the tent, and half of the chairs were taken when we arrived. On one side in the front row were a few handcarved chodrums, 18 inches tall, 3 feet long, and 1 foot wide. They had ornate Buddhist motifs carved into the sides, and on top were cushions covered with handwoven textiles. Each chodrum was large enough for two people, and the chodrums were reserved for VIPs. In the middle of the seating area was a swath of grass on which the women dancers from the night before were again performing traditional dances. Meanwhile, servants were walking around with trays of snacks and bowls of betel nuts.

Instead of sitting, Carrie, Linda, and I walked to the end of the tent to the buffet, and were delighted to find huge trays of ema datse, grilled pork, and fresh trout. In the center of the table sat a big bowl of something that looked very unfamiliar, but which someone told me was *gin-ngyem*.

What's gin-ngyem? I peered into the bowl, which was filled with a gooey pile of minuscule critters resembling tiny fried shrimp. But they couldn't have been shrimp. Bhutan is landlocked and doesn't have shrimp. I looked closer. What were these dark creatures with torpedo-shaped bodies and wings?

"Check this out!" I said to Carrie, who was pushing Claudia in her stroller. "I think these are cooked bees."

"No," said a Bhutanese woman. "They're hornets."

"Don't touch them!" Carrie shrieked.

Ignoring her, I scooped some hornets onto my plate and dangled a spoonful in front of my mouth. I still wasn't sure if I was going to eat them, but I knew just holding the gin-ngyem by my mouth would make Carrie freak out. "No, you'll get sick!" said Carrie.

"It's nice to know you love me," I said.

A Bhutanese man standing next to us smiled and heaped a spoonful onto his plate. "This is one of the rarest delicacies in Bhutan," he said. "It's good luck, like Viagra."

The hornets that are used in gin-ngyem are bred in farms. Killing the hornets is an illegal act according to Buddhist tradition because it involves taking the life of a sentient being, but in Bhutan, the taste buds often trump the religious conscience, and the hornets are so rich in protein that they're also given to pregnant women and used in some traditional medicines. (If you want to make gin-ngyem, here's a brief recipe Habu gave me: Sauté hornets in a heap of butter; add lots of garlic and ginger and a little chili powder; garnish with green onion leaves.)

"You'd better take some, because this will be the first dish to go," the man said.

I was queasy, but I couldn't back off. Not after taunting Carrie. I pushed the spoon into my mouth and chewed the hornets. They were crunchy, delicate, and sweet, kind of like a succulent soft-shell crab. "Delicious," I exclaimed.

I tried to put a scoop onto Carrie's plate, but she pushed back my hand. "No way," she said.

By eleven o'clock the tent was full and people were gaily eating and softly chatting. Suddenly everybody stood and the tent was silent. Habu got up from one of the chodrums and scampered over to the tent's entrance, where a small phalanx of husky men in ghos were standing in two parallel lines, forming a human tunnel. I assumed the new husband and wife would arrive, but instead, a tiny and frail old monk, hunched forward at the waist, gingerly walked inside. His face was wrinkled and tan; he had a full head of shiny gray hair clipped short in a crew cut; and he was wearing an airy maroon monk's robe with a yellow shawl. The monk slowly made a circuit of the tent, his guards at his sides, and softly tossed blessings with his hands to each guest in the front row.

When the monk passed us, I noticed that one of the body-guards was carrying a small white poodle. When the monk finally reached his chodrum, the guard prostrated and put the poodle down next to the monk, and the monk patted the dog. I leaned over to a Bhutanese man next to me. "Who's that monk?" I asked.

"The je khenpo," he replied.

"Who's that?" I asked.

The je khenpo, he politely explained, is the head of Bhutan's monk body and the second most powerful person in Bhutan be-hind the king, a status noted by the yellow shawl, which only the king and the je khenpo wear over their ghos and robes. The je khenpo holds a unique position among Buddhist leaders around the world, because he ascends to his post not by reincar-nation, and not as a child, but as an adult who's selected based on meritorious service. (By contrast, most other Buddhist lead-ers, including the Dalai Lama, are anointed as reincarnates by fellow monks when they're very young children, sometimes just two or three years old.)

The je khenpo here today, eighty-two-year-old Ngawang Thinley Lhundup, was no longer in office. He was Bhutan's sixty-seventh and longest-reigning je khenpo, in power from 1970 to 1986. Since retiring, he had reportedly passed time by meditating and performing religious ceremonies.

It seemed like most guests were watching the dancers, proba-bly because the dancers were right in front of them and there was no other entertainment, but I was transfixed by the je khenpo. He sat so serenely, his palms resting on his knees, as he observed the dancers. Suddenly the poodle jumped off the bench and ran into the circle of dancing women. Nobody said a word or laughed, and the dancers didn't break their rhythm for a second, but I had to hold back laughter as the poodle scampered around the grass. After a couple of moments he found his way back to the bench, but just before reaching the je khenpo the poodle slid to a stop by a wooden pole holding up the tent. The poodle lifted one of his back legs and urinated on the pole. Finally this was too much and I exhaled a few chuckles, but as I was chuckling, Carrie whipped around and slapped a hand over my mouth.

"That's like laughing at God!" she whispered.

The poodle coolly sauntered back to the je khenpo's chodrum, cocky as Jack Nicholson at the Oscars, and jumped back up next to the je khenpo. Then the je khenpo leaned over and began petting his pooch.

By noon, the dancing was over and the je khenpo had left, and in his wake, the crowd filtered out of the tent and into the driveway. We got on line to enter Habu's house and officially greet the bride and groom, who were in the prayer room where they were married. I ran down the driveway to our Land Cruiser to get our wedding gift, a rice cooker we bought in Thimphu.

When we entered the prayer room, I was overwhelmed by the multitude of colorful Buddhist images and artifacts adorning every square inch of the walls, floor, shelves, and ceiling. Kuenzang Dem, the bride, and Sonam Phuntsho, the groom, were at the opposite end of the room from which we had entered. They were next to each other, kneeling on large square pillows with a chodrum in front of them. Guests formed a line that stretched along one wall and past the newlyweds. When we reached the couple, Linda, Carrie, and I bowed and I held out our gift, which Sonam Phuntsho put behind him on a huge pile of presents that included, in addition to several other rice cookers, toaster ovens, blenders, silverware, baby toys, sheets and blankets, and lots of other things for the house.

"Looks like you guys got as many useless gifts, at least as far as a guy is concerned, as we got at our wedding," I said to Sonam Phuntsho.

He chuckled. "It's not about me. It's about my wife," Sonam Phuntsho said.

"You've been well trained," I said.

Kuenzang Dem gently laughed.

"How long have you been sitting here?" I asked.

"Too long," Sonam Phuntsho said. "It seems like we've been in this room since yesterday morning. I'm hot and tired. It's certainly more fun being a guest at a Bhutanese wedding than being the husband and wife."

WE PASSED THE afternoon shuttling between the tent and the courtyard, basking in the sunshine and talking with our Bhutanese friends. Indeed, many of the guests were members at Royal Thimphu who sat in lawn chairs drinking Tiger beer (an import from Singapore) and lamenting how the wedding caused them to miss a day of golf. I asked a couple of the men where their wives were, and they both said their spouses were back in Thimphu. Not surprising, because married Bhutanese men and women often socialize without their spouses.

"Why'd you choose the wedding over golf?" I asked.

"Gotta pay respects to Dasho [Habu], who is a great man," said Leki Dorji. "But it would've been much more fun to be on the course."

Habu walked over and with a wide grin bellowed, "Linda, baby. Are you having fun? Tonight we'll get the real music cooking and everybody will be dancing."

AT ABOUT THREE P.M. we returned to the Y.T. Lodge to rest and shower before the final night's festivities. We were back at the wedding by seven, and Habu was there again to welcome us. "Linda, baby," Habu said. "I'm so happy you came. Let's have a drink and dance."

Linda blushed while holding Claudia. "Maybe later," Linda said. "I'll just help take care of Claudia for now."

"Could we visit the dzong tonight?" I asked.

"How about now?" Habu said.

A few minutes later, one of Habu's servants was leading us up a tall and steep stone staircase at the front of the dzong. The servant unlocked the padlock and pushed open one of the two huge wooden doors, each 15 feet tall, 6 feet wide, and 6 inches thick. We entered and he closed the door, and as we strolled into the courtyard with an oak tree in the middle of it I was struck by the silence. It was such a contrast to the blaring rock music at the wedding party outside. A few chickens and dogs were sleeping around the oak tree. The full moon's light illuminated the slabs of slate on the floor, and my eyes were drawn to the long shadow of the tree. A couple of young monks, perhaps ten years old, wearing red robes and flip-flops, scurried across the courtyard.

"We go to disco," said one of the monks.

"Party," his friend added.

"You going to the wedding?" Carrie asked.

The boys smiled and laughed and ran off.

Two years ago, as tourists, Carrie and I stood in this courtyard at four-thirty A.M. during the Wangdi tsechu, the town's annual religious festival. We were there so early to watch the year's most sacred religious event in Wangdi, the unfurling in the dzong of the Wangdi monkhood's 100-foot-tall silk and cotton thangka. Predawn unfurlings of oversized thangkas are done at most tsechus, and hordes of villagers attend the events to pay respects to their Buddhist deities and gain positive karma. As a tourist, I remembered feeling like an outsider at the unfurling, but during this second visit I felt at home in the courtyard amid the intoxicatingly mystical silence.

Habu's servant led us on a tour of the dzong, taking us by the district's administrative offices surrounding the courtyard and then into the back of the dzong where the monks lived, worked, and went to school. In one large prayer room, a gaggle of teenage monks sat cross-legged on the smooth wood-plank floor, reciting prayers, while another gaggle of monks played cards, chewed gum, and blew bubbles. In another prayer room there was a lone monk sitting cross-legged with his back against a wall, fast asleep.

AT EIGHT O'CLOCK, back outside the dzong, the tent was roaring with music from a boom box and guests were dancing and singing. Claudia might have been the happiest person in the tent. She was wearing a powder blue jumpsuit and a pink ski hat, and she spent the next half hour on the dance floor, being passed from one Bhutanese to another.

"We should charge ten dollars per dance," I said to Linda.

Linda danced with Y.T. and she smiled widely, watching

Habu dance with her granddaughter. "It's like a fraternity party," Linda said.

At about nine, Claudia suddenly started wailing, a sure sign that she was tired. I mixed some baby formula and mineral water, fed Claudia a bottle, and put her in her stroller. After walking her around the courtyard for a few minutes, Claudia calmed down and I rolled the stroller back into the tent. "She's a trooper," Habu said.

A little later I noticed a lithe young man wearing a flowing light gray silk robe, or cape, and smooth black leather shoes. He had a very short crew cut and gold wire-rim glasses. I suspected he was a monk, perhaps a lama. His robe was shaped just like a monk's robe, and he had an aura of deep serenity, as if he was meditating, which was a startling contrast to the booming music and gyrating bodies filling the dance area we were standing by. I approached him and said, "Hello, I'm the golf coach."

"Yes, I know," he replied gently. His voice was smooth, measured, and peaceful, as if he has just emerged from meditating. "You do good works for our country."

How did he know me? Who was he?

"I'm Iron Bridge," he said.

Wow! I knew *that* name. He was the reincarnated lama described in the Lonely Planet guidebook. Reportedly he's the thirteenth reincarnation of a Tibetan saint who built 108 bridges in Tibet and Bhutan in the fifteenth century. This was *very* cool. Over the years, and especially since coming to Bhutan, I'd seen them portrayed in movies and heard so much about reincarnated monks—about their mystical histories, their great abilities to commune with the heavens, and their tranquil demeanors. But to be honest, I'd always been a bit skeptical about reincarnated monks, because I didn't believe in reincarnation. At least I didn't believe in it until meeting Iron Bridge.

Carrie and I were excited to meet such an intriguing person, and we peppered Iron Bridge with questions. He was eloquent and engaging, even a bit funny. "I was discovered at fifteen, in the Paro dzong where I was a monk," he said. "The Dalai Lama's representative came by, and a divination told him that I was Iron Bridge."

"What did you think when you found out who you were?" I asked.

"I was very happy," Iron Bridge said.

"What does it feel like to be reincarnated?" I said.

Iron Bridge paused. He picked up Claudia from her stroller and held her so tenderly that Claudia looked as happy and serene as ever. Iron Bridge was thinking, perhaps meditating, searching for an answer. The silence was not tense; it was sweet and relaxed. He continued, "I am very content."

After leaving Paro with the Dalai Lama's people, Iron Bridge spent a dozen years learning and meditating in India under the Dalai Lama. Now Iron Bridge was thirty years old, married, and the father of an eighteen-month-old daughter. (Apparently you can be a monk and be married.) He lived with his wife and child on the outskirts of Thimphu at his private monastery, where he routinely hosts members of his worldwide following of devotees. He was at the wedding because Habu is his father-in-law. "I'm coming to America to see my people in a couple of months," Iron Bridge said.

"Perhaps we could see you then." Carrie said.

Iron Bridge pulled out a business card that had his e-mail and fax. "That would be very nice, if I am not too busy."

This was exceedingly strange. I was a bit in awe. Here was a reincarnated monk, somebody whom I'd read about and imagined to be something ethereal. But, in fact, Iron Bridge was quite down-to-earth, easy to talk to, and he had a business card. Encounters involving such unusual things—unusual to me, a New Yorker, anyway—seemed to happen regularly in Bhutan, and I loved them, because they made me feel like I was living in a dream.

I imagined I was back in New York playing golf. I'm walking down the fairway with my friends and trying to tell them what happened at the wedding in Bhutan. I begin to talk, telling them, "You'll never guess who I met. *A reincarnated monk who does e-mail and has a fax and a business card.*"

Then I imagined my friends' reaction. Blank faces. Disbelief. Then they burst into sarcastic laughter. "Yeah, right, Rick," one friend says. "Let me guess: You also played golf with Sasquatch in Bhutan."

The friends walk away to hit their shots. They don't believe a word I've said.

Back in the tent with Iron Bridge, I wondered if this was a dream. Was he pulling my leg? Or was he sincere? There was no indication that he was anything but the genuine article.

"How much do you meditate?" I asked.

Iron Bridge had a little smile. He seemed to be enjoying our talk. "I meditated for eight straight months last year," he said.

"Without a break?" Carrie asked.

"Of course," he replied.

Of course. Eight consecutive months in one room in some monastery high in the Himalayas. That's something everybody can relate to. Maybe everybody from Bhutan, but not where I come from. Iron Bridge was so matter-of-fact and sincere as he told me about himself, but his words were jarring my mind, in a good way.

Iron Bridge was still holding Claudia. She was smiling as contentedly as I'd ever seen. She was definitely charmed. Had my daughter found her soul mate?

"*Chey chey*," said Iron Bridge, looking directly in Claudia's blue eyes.

"Is that some Buddhist term?" I asked.

Iron Bridge smiled. He spoke to me but continued looking at Claudia. "No, no," he said. "It's an affection for little ones. You might say, 'Darling one.'"

Iron Bridge passed Claudia back to Carrie. "I should be going now," he said.

"I hope we can get together again," I said.

"Yes, yes, that would be my pleasure," Iron Bridge said.

"Did you ever play golf?" I said.

"No. I only have time to meditate," Iron Bridge replied.

"Maybe you'll play in your next life," I said.

Iron Bridge had a wry grin. "Will you teach me?" he said.

I thought: Was Iron Bridge assuming that I was going to be reincarnated, too? Was he assuming that we were going to meet in our next lives? Did he know something I didn't?

"Do you think I could be a good golfer?" asked Iron Bridge.

"No doubt," I said, and I was being honest.

MINUTES AFTER IRON BRIDGE walked off, Carrie, Linda, and I ventured out to dance as I was holding Claudia in my arms. About fifteen Bhutanese were twisting and turning on the matted grass as Shakira songs blasted from the boom box on the table that had been filled with the buffet twelve hours earlier. It was interesting to see the vast array of ages out there dancing: there were sixty-year-old men and teenagers.

A middle-aged man with a mustache and a gho wiggled over to Carrie, Linda, and me and joined our little dancing circle. He said hello and told us his name, but I couldn't understand it. The music was too loud and his voice was slurred, perhaps from imbibing too much of the home-brewed *ara*, or rice wine. We all exchanged small talk while dancing.

Linda came over to me and put out her arms. She wanted to dance with Claudia, whose eyes sparkled with joy when I passed her to Grandma. But Claudia wasn't as happy as Linda, who began dancing more intensely, shifting and turning while beaming a smile brighter than I had ever seen on her freckled face. Linda was babbling baby talk to Claudia and smiling right into her eyes.

"So was it worth it, trekking all the way from Great Neck to Bhutan?" I asked, looking at Linda.

Linda turned her gaze toward me. I was just a couple feet away. She was turning to and fro, moving to the music, and cuddling Claudia. A warm, sure smile washed over Linda's face. She didn't have to say a word.

Chapter 13

JHOMOLHARI, HERE WE COME

COMPARED TO THE rest of Bhutan, Thimphu seems like a booming metropolis, and on my trek to Jhomolhari, I was feeling a bit of withdrawal from Thimphu's relatively go-go urbanity—barking dogs, car horns, new construction, Internet cafés, and restaurants. It was nine-thirty P.M., and I was a full day's walk into the Bhutanese wilderness. Above was a black sky teeming with stars. The only sounds were the rush of glacier-cold water whirring down the river just below our campsite, and wind rustling through the pine trees.

"*This* is gross national happiness," said Chuck Yash.

I agreed, with one exception: "We stink," I said. The campsite was redolent of Vaseline, sweat, mud, and malodorous socks, pants, hats, and gloves hanging on a string by our tent. Redeeming the atmosphere slightly was the lingering smell of the succulent chicken curry and red rice we'd eaten for dinner.

Chuck, a hale man in his early fifties, lived in Rancho Santa Fe, California. A graduate of the U.S. Naval Academy and Harvard Business School and a Vietnam veteran, he had recently retired as the president of Callaway Golf, the last stop in a distinguished career in the golf industry. Before retiring, Chuck, a single-digit handicapper and longtime business friend, arranged for Callaway to donate clubs, balls, bags, and clothes for my teaching program in Bhutan, and once Chuck left Callaway, he decided to come to Bhutan and work for a month as my teaching assistant.

Chuck and I were sitting outside the tent that we were sharing on our weeklong trek to the 14,000-foot base camp of Jhomolhari, a 23,996-foot-tall mountain in the northwestern corner of Bhutan that is the country's most sacred peak. Also trekking with us and sharing another tent were the younger of Chuck's two daughters, Meagan, a junior at UC Santa Clara who had taken a leave from school, and Camilla Bang, a Danish friend from Thimphu who was living in Bhutan with her husband, Martin, while he completed an assignment with UNICEF.

Chuck and I were exhausted but thrilled. After teaching golf from dawn to dusk, seven days a week, we were finally taking a break and getting a glimpse of the rest of Bhutan. It was even more beautiful than I'd imagined. The only other place I had trekked, Nepal, had floored me with its bigger-than-life snow-capped mountains, but Nepal doesn't have nearly as many rivers as Bhutan, nor does it have as many lush, bottomless valleys that twist and turn like snakes. Also, most trekking areas in Nepal are inhabited only by teahouse proprietors and other people who cater to tourists. In Bhutan, treks wind through magical little high-altitude farming villages that are virtually the same as they were centuries ago.

Trekking in Bhutan was also easier than I'd expected. Our trail climbed at a surprisingly mild gradient, at least for the Himalayas, and it had been worn smooth by the traffic of mountain dwellers shuttling goods to and from Paro. But what really made the trek seem easy was the pampered way we were traveling. We each carried only a small backpack with water, snacks, and sunscreen, because the $75-a-day fee we paid Sonam Kesang to arrange this jaunt included a trekking staff. We had a guide, an assistant guide, two cooks, two horsemen, and a dozen pack-horses to lug our mountain of gear, which included propane tanks for cooking, golf clubs and balls, a Porta Potti tent, dozens of fresh eggs, canned orange juice, and bottled beer.

We started walking at eight o'clock in the morning at the Drukgyel dzong, a dilapidated stone fort at the mouth of the serpentine valley that begins in Paro and snakes up to Jhomolhari. Built in 1649, the dzong was devastated in 1951 when a butter lamp spilled and caused a massive fire, and the damage has never been repaired.

The mountain passes along the Bhutan–Tibet border around Jhomolhari are relatively low (up to 20,000 feet, which is sky-high to most people, but not to Himalayan dwellers), and that has made the valley a key juncture for activity between Tibet and Bhutan. Over the past few centuries Tibet has tried several times to mount invasions through the valley, sending troops by Jhomolhari and down the Paro River Valley into Bhutan. Most of the time, the Bhutanese militia waited in Paro and used the Drukgyel dzong as its base, and the Bhutanese have always thwarted the Tibetans—and everyone else who tried to invade, for that matter, including the British, who tried without success to invade Bhutan from its southern border in 1864. The Bhutanese are fiercely proud of their record in war, and as a result of its military success, the kingdom, unlike most of its South Asian neighbors, has never been colonized. "The last time the Tibetans came [in 1644] we hid in the dzong and did a surprise attack when they arrived,"

Pema, our trekking guide, said. "We destroyed them. Chopped off many heads. And the survivors turned around and ran home."

Despite the occasional skirmishes, the Bhutan–Tibet border has long been a key bartering route between the two countries. The Bhutanese offer things hard to find and manufacture in Tibet, especially food such as rice and potatoes, while the Tibetans provide the Bhutanese with household goods such as plastic dishes, shoes, and electronics.

The first few hours of our walk we traveled along a gushing river and through several farming villages. The villages had no stores, roads, or town centers. Rather, each village comprised dozens of square miles of farmland divided among several families. The village center was simply a cluster of houses perched where the corners of the farmland met. The villagers keep the houses close together for reasons both practical—families share supplies and the children form groups to walk together to and from school—and social, because without clustering, families would have to walk for hours just to see other human beings.

We walked by farmers toiling amid chest-high golden rice stalks, terraced fields, and paddies, all shadowed by enormous mountains. Some of the farmers were hunched over and harvesting rice by hand, while others were turning over dirt by guiding plows pulled by water buffalos. It was idyllic to pass through, and I was constantly reminded of Impressionist paintings, including Van Gogh's *Haystacks*. But the farmers' deeply calloused hands, permanently soiled clothes, and faces so wrinkled and weather-beaten that people who looked like they were sixty years old were probably forty, conspired to illustrate that these people's lives were brutally hard.

"How do the farmers survive year after year?" I asked Pema.

"They know nothing else," said Pema. "Yes, they work too

hard. But they have no obligations and support themselves. These people might be happier than those of us who have left the villages to work in Thimphu."

Pema grew up in the far eastern side of Bhutan, in a village where the men are farmers and the women are weavers who produce many of the kingdom's most valuable textiles, many of them exquisite silk ghos and kiras. "It was a simple life, but a happy life I had in my village," said Pema as we strolled along the trail under bright sunlight. "There were no worries because there are no wants. But now in Thimphu it is always a struggle and everybody wants more, more, more."

After eight hours on the trail, the valley narrowed considerably, and we came to a small military base. There were a few barracks; a large, dusty sports field used for training and athletics; and some offices. A group of fifty high schoolers divided into two parallel lines—one for boys and one for girls—marched around the field and loudly sang the Bhutanese national anthem in Dzongkha to prepare for a performance on the king's birthday, November 11, which was a few weeks away. On the birthday, every city and village in the kingdom has a major celebration, with dancing, singing, and lots of processional marching.

Next to the sports field was a dirt basketball court with schoolboys playing on it. The boys were wearing ghos and tattered black dress shoes and flip-flops; not one child had sneakers. It was fun to watch the kids zigzag around while dribbling, passing, and shooting with unbridled joy. After one boy swished a shot through the netless hoop, I clapped.

"You're Michael Jordan!" I said.

The boy smiled and shrugged his shoulders with a blank look on his face. Basketball had reached the roof of the world, but marketing had not.

When we walked into camp at about six-thirty P.M., all the tents—two for sleeping, one for dining, and another for a toilet— were set up, and dinner was cooking. Our trekking staff had arrived hours before us, and our assistant guide, Dawala, brought us two large steel pots of boiling water to wash up. Half an hour later we were in the dining tent feasting on curried chicken, red rice, and boiled asparagus. Each plate was garnished with long, narrow slices of tomato skins shaped like hearts.

"It's like Le Cirque du Jhomolhari," I said as Chuck, Camilla, Meagan, and I ate by candlelight in the dining tent at a fold-up plastic table covered by a red-and-white-checkered tablecloth.

"It's too good," said Camilla. "I might gain weight out here."

ON THE MORNING of day two, I was awakened at six A.M. by what people at sea level refer to as the call of nature. But as I lay in my goose-down sleeping bag, it became obvious that up here, nature has another call, and it was telling me loud and clear to stay right where I was. Even inside the tent, it was so cold that I could see my breath, and the two slats of the angled roof were covered with frost. I imagined the rescue squad finding my body frozen upright, my zipper half undone. Chuck, meanwhile, was out cold, purring like a baby. (I wish he purred at night, too; his snoring concerto from last night was still ringing in my ears.)

Finally, with my bladder about to burst, I pulled on some fleece pants, a shell jacket, and a ski cap and braved the cold. Outside, it was not nearly as murderous as I'd thought, so after my pit stop, I ambled down to the river and sat on a silky-smooth round boulder the size of a VW Beetle.

The water, moving hard and fast, was perhaps 15 feet deep and full of large rocks and felled trees. I followed a big brown leaf careening atop the water and spinning in circles until it was sucked under the surface and disappeared. I couldn't see any fish, although the night before Pema told us that the river had trout like those I'd eaten at the wedding. I couldn't help but think about something very strange: Many Bhutanese, especially people in Thimphu, have never enjoyed the blissful beauty I was experiencing. Why? "Trekking, oh, that would be hard!" said one teenager who attended my youth clinics. Odd as that sounds coming from somebody who lives in the Himalayas, it's a common refrain in Bhutan. Indeed, many Bhutanese have never trekked or hiked. Perhaps, though, I shouldn't have been surprised. I know lots of New Yorkers, starting with yours truly, who've never been to Ellis Island.

After an hour by the river, I headed back to the campsite to find Chuck, Camilla, and Meagan sitting at the plastic dining table, having a sumptuous breakfast. Splayed out were dishes containing pancakes, scrambled eggs, porridge, toast (with jelly and butter), and containers of orange juice and coffee. "Bhutan doesn't have chain stores, but who needs them? This is better than IHOP," I said.

We hit the trail at eight-thirty A.M. After a few minutes the military base barracks looked tiny, and a few minutes later we were deep in the woods and the base was lost behind us. That's one of the eerie things about walking in the Himalayas: Something dominates your field of vison one minute, and it's vanished into oblivion the next.

At about ten-thirty we took a break by a log cabin with a porch and some big antennas on the roof. "A communications depot for the army," said Pema. There were two men on the benches; one was a diminutive Bhutanese and the other a tall, slender

European. Their names were Sangay Dawa, a civil engineer with the Bhutanese Ministry of Health, and Thomas Jorgenson, a Danish engineering consultant in Dawa's office. They were returning from a typical Bhutanese business trip: a six-day trek on foot to do maintenance work on the community health center in Lingzhi, a vast and uneven plateau that's a day's walk past the Jhomolhari base camp.

At 15,000 feet above sea level, Lingzhi is one of the most isolated yet populous mountain communities in Bhutan, home to flocks of blue sheep and musk deer and about a thousand people, most of them nomads, farmers, and yak herders. The community, just miles from the Tibetan border, is known for three things: its beautiful dzong, originally built at the end of the seventeenth century; its plentiful herbs, which in summer are harvested and made into medicines that are used throughout Bhutan; and its mailman, Ugyen Tenzin.

Tenzin is a legend in Bhutan. According to *Kuensel*, Tenzin has been making the eight-day round-trip trek from Lingzhi to Thimphu to deliver and retrieve mail since 1976. Buoyed by his $100 monthly salary from the Bhutan Postal Corporation, Tenzin travels alone with his pet horse, Norbu, and is fearless despite the intense rigors of his job (tigers and bears abound along the trail to Thimphu). "For me, it is not about carrying letters or delivering packages," Tenzin told *Kuensel*. "It is about doing something for my community, about trust, about bearing good news for others. Sometimes they [the residents of Lingzhi] are so happy to see me they treat me to grand meals."

I was reminded of Tenzin on the trail this morning when we were passed by a caravan of men, women, and children returning to Lingzhi. Most of these people were wearing flip-flops, a stark contrast to my hiking boots, but what really awed me was watching the men lug sheets of corrugated metal, each 8 feet by 4 feet, on their backs. "The metal is for roofs on their homes," said Pema. "They went down to Paro to get it."

On his back, each man had two pieces of metal held together by a rope that hung over one shoulder so he could keep the load steady as he walked.

"Each piece weighs 30 kilos," Pema said.

"Holy cow," said Chuck. "How do they carry so much?"

"They have no choice," said Pema.

Chuck laughed in amazement. "The next time I go to Home Depot, I'll definitely remember these guys."

AT FIVE-THIRTY P.M., just a short walk outside our campsite, Pema abruptly waved us to run up into the woods off the trail and yelled, "Up, up, go up! Sit and wait!"

"What's happening?" asked Meagan.

"Angry yaks!" Pema said.

I chuckled for a split second. "Angry yaks" had a comic ring, at least to my ears, but the smile quickly vanished, replaced by fright. A moment later I heard grunting and clanging bells, and soon after that I saw two herders, both men, leading a pack of five humongous black-and-white beasts down the trail. The herders were holding them back with thick ropes, but the yaks were lunging to and fro, like bulls behind bars, in a desperate attempt to break free. They harrumphed through a stream, making huge splashes, but one monster stopped in the water, turned his head to us, and glared. We were 30 feet away, up from the path, but I clearly saw the yak's bulging eyes, glutinous snot, and sharp horns.

"He'd make a great carpet," I said. "I haven't had a shag in my house since freshman year at college."

Pema laughed. "I'd like to have him for dinner," he said.

"This will be a world record!" yelled Chuck, surveying his tee shot on the par 3. He had a wedge in his hand and 80 yards to the flagstick, a twig with a few sheets of toilet paper wrapped around the top of it. The stick was in a hand-dug hole and fluttering in the stiff breeze, while Chuck's ball, a pearly white Top Flite, sat on a pile of bone-dry yak dung.

"It'll be the highest hole in one ever!" said Chuck.

Alas, Chuck didn't make an ace. His ball landed 10 yards short of the flag, bounced off a couple of rocks, rolled over some twigs, and caromed into another pile of yak dung—this one was wet and spongy—six feet from the cup. But the errant shot didn't disappoint, and Chuck received a standing ovation from the gallery, which included Pema, Meagan, Camilla, our cooks, the two horsemen, some trekking staff from another group, and me. "Nice shot, Dad," said Meagan.

It was our lunch break during day three, and we were finally playing the first golf of our trek. I had been anxiously waiting to find an open space in which we could use the clubs our horses had been carrying. Now, after walking for four hours with our mouths agape from the sun-drenched mountain scenery, we stopped on wide-open tundra at 12,000 feet. Chuck and I each had a wedge and some golf balls, and we were hitting shots across the tundra.

At first the trekking staffers stood looking perplexed. "Strange game," said Dawala.

"Very interesting game," said Pema. "It looks like a good challenge."

Like most Bhutanese, these guys had never played golf, and their only acquaintance with the game were the sightings of it they'd had passing by Royal Thimphu.

"Hit a shot," I said to Pema while holding out my club for him.

"No, sir," Pema said. "It's your vacation."

"Come on, hit one," Chuck said.

Pema sheepishly grabbed the wedge. Without any guidance, he stood up to the ball and took some practice swings, which were surprisingly well balanced.

"You're a quick study," said Chuck.

After a dozen practice swings, Pema hit a shot, and it was a beauty. The ball flew about 100 yards, and Pema and his peers on our trekking staff were converted into instant golf addicts, playing for the rest of the lunch break and during every spare moment for the rest of the trek. They even became teachers, giving lessons to the trekking staff of other groups that camped near us.

During the afternoon, we walked up a narrow valley and along a river. We passed farms, a schoolhouse, a health center, and a few herds of grazing yaks. The visual highlights, though, were what the Bhutanese call "blue sheep," formally known as bharal. With dense, short, slate-gray fur that looks pale blue from afar, they travel in packs of up to eighty between 9,000 and 20,000 feet. Both males and females have curvaceous horns, and the males can reach 3 feet in height.

We arrived at our campsite at four P.M. After just a few days, we were moving faster; this day's trek, which covered about 10 miles, took seven hours, which was ninety minutes less than the first two days'. Our camp was in a yak-herding settlement called Jangothang, reputedly one of the most stunning sites in all of the Himalayas. On a flat valley floor comprised of tundra bisected by a huge river, Jangothang sits at 14,000 feet, an altitude I'd reached just once before—during my honeymoon in the fall of 1995, when Carrie and I trekked to the Annapurna base camp in the Annapurna Sanctuary in Nepal.

What makes the Jhomolhari base camp so jaw-dropping is its proximity to the towering snowcapped mountains and glaciers that bridge the area between the valley floor and the mountains. Indeed, Jhomolhari and Jichu Drakye, the two largest peaks in the area, were so close to the base camp that I felt like I could tee up a driver and launch a ball into the snowy slopes.

We were standing atop the walls of a burned-out rock fortress that Pema said was likely used by Bhutanese warriors centuries ago during their battles against the Tibetans. Today the decrepit fortress is just a terrific place to take pictures and a fun place to tee up a golf ball, which I did. My shot was a good one, the ball taking a high, long arc and disappearing against the snowy-white backdrop. Pema was impressed.

"You must be professional," Pema said.

Chuck laughed. "A professional writer," he said.

"Has anybody ever been up to the summit?" I asked.

"Yes, I've heard stories about an expedition. Bhutanese and Indians, I think," Pema replied. "Some of them reached the summit of Jhomolhari. But then the weather got bad and there was death."

"What happened?" I asked.

"I'm not sure," Pema replied. "I just know the villagers around here believed the gods were angry, so they asked the government to stop the climbers."

"Did they?" asked Chuck.

"Yes," said Pema. "I think that was the end of mountaineering in Bhutan."

Banning mountaineering in Bhutan is like banning surfing in Hawaii, but preserving culture comes first in Bhutan, even if that means sacrificing millions of dollars in potential tourist revenue.

"I think one of the survivors, a man in the army, is still alive," said Pema.

"Do you think we can find that man when we go back to Thimphu?" I asked.

"We can try," said Pema.

Pema's story stirred my mind and made me crave more information. It seemed like he had revealed the tip of the iceberg for what could be a fascinating story. If the man Pema referred to was indeed alive, I was going to find him.

AFTER DINNER, AT about six P.M., Pema and Dawala set up a nine-hole course on the valley floor using twig and toilet-paper flagsticks. The first tee was next to the cooking area, and our group included about eight guys and Camilla, a 15-handicapper, while Meagan followed us and took pictures.

"What should we call the course?" I said.

"Yak Dung Club," our cook said.

Laughter all around.

We played for ninety minutes. It was chilly enough to see your breath, about thirty-five degrees, and we were all wearing ski caps, but the nip didn't dampen anybody's enthusiasm. We were having too much fun. Balls caromed off rocks and into streams. They landed in yak dung. At one hole, a guide with another group ricocheted a chip off the buttocks of one of our horsemen. (Thankfully, the horseman wasn't hurt.) At another hole, Dawala took six putts from just 3 feet, but when the ball trickled into the dirt hole he was ecstatic and threws his arms skyward.

"You're a Bhutanese Tiger Woods," I told Dawala.

"Yes," said Ugyen Dorji, the twenty-one-year-old guide for another group of trekkers staying at the base camp. "We will call him Tiger Dawala."

One thing I love about golf is that you can learn a lot about somebody while playing with him, and that was true even on our makeshift course at base camp. I befriended Ugyen as we played, and the more we talked, the more I was intrigued. Like so many young Bhutanese, Ugyen wanted to see the world beyond Bhutan, but he didn't have the money. Ugyen also harbored dreams of athletic fame, even though the only athletes who've ever made a living in Bhutan are archers on the national team, and their meager monthly stipend of $200 is comparable to a schoolteacher's salary. But Ugyen's most interesting passion was literature. His favorite book from school was *The Merchant of Venice*. "I was Shylock in the class performance," said Ugyen.

"You've read a lot of Shakespeare?" I asked.

"Yes, I like his work very much," said Ugyen. "My other favorite is *As You Like It*, because it's a love story. I especially like Orlando."

The list of unexpected surprises got longer that evening. At about nine, Chuck, Camilla, Meagan, and I were having fresh popcorn and lounging in the meal tent when Pema, nattily dressed in jeans and a button-down oxford underneath his down parka, entered the tent. "You guys want to dance?" he asked.

We all chuckled. "Sure," said Chuck sardonically. "Are you taking us to the Jangothang disco?"

By now Chuck should've known not to underestimate the Bhutanese. Of course Jangothang didn't have a disco. It didn't have electricity, and only a few nomadic families lived in the area. But the base camp had a stone guest hut that trekkers and guides from another group had turned into a high-altitude Studio 54. They used candles for light, an MP3 player and two hand-size speakers for music, and the refreshments included bottles of rum and vodka and thermoses of hot tea. Outside it was freezing, literally, but inside it was cooking. The scene was almost too surreal for words as our group, some trekkers from Sweden, and the various trekking guides, cooks, and horsemen danced while wearing ski parkas and wool caps.

Ugyen was particularly inspired. When a Bob Marley song played, he gyrated and waved his arms, yelling, "Yeah, man, I love the ganja master!"

Then the hit song "Whenever, Wherever," by Shakira, played. "She has a nice ass and just shakes it all the time," Ugyen blithely said.

The next song was "Hotel California," by the Eagles, and everybody chanted, "Livin' it up at the Hotel Jhomolhari."

After a while Pema turned off the MP3, and the Bhutanese men formed a circle, joined hands, and began singing Bhutanese folk songs. At first Chuck, Meagan, Camilla, the Swedes, and I stood back and watched, but then Pema asked us to join the circle.

The atmosphere in the hut calmed dramatically, but my inspiration level rose. The gentle voices of the Bhutanese and the pretty songs they were singing resonated in a beautiful way, giving me goose bumps. I didn't understand a word they were singing, because they were singing in Dzongkha, but I felt the unity and deep devotion embedded in the songs. I was also moved by the fact that everybody had joined hands and we were gracefully rotating in a clockwise direction.

I couldn't help but think of a comment the chief justice had made to me back in Thimphu about gross national happiness.

He said that GNH would not be successful if people were happy just by themselves; GNH, he said, must cause the people of the kingdom to be happy together. "It is gross *national* happiness," he said, "not gross individual happiness."

I thought the unity nurtured up here was a good example of what the chief justice hoped for with GNH.

SADLY, OUR PARTY—the trek—ended two days later. We reluctantly broke camp on our final morning and savored our last breakfast of fresh over-easy fried eggs, crisp toast, and steaming porridge served to us at a little plastic table in an idyllic Himalayan setting. We then spent the first few hours of the day heading down the same path from the base camp we had taken up, passing the same farms we had seen on the first morning.

At about noon we rounded a corner shrouded by tall, wispy grass, and I saw the Drukgyel dzong. Soon I heard the buzz of motor vehicles and of people talking on the street in front of the few shops near the dzong.

"Back to civilization," I said, pausing. "Well, maybe it's away from it."

"I'm not sure whether we're going to or from civilization," said Chuck. "But I wish we were walking in the other direction."

Chapter 14

DEATH ON THE SUMMIT

O N   T H E   S U M M I T of Jhomolhari, Lieutenant Chachu of
the Bhutanese Army wondered when he'd take his last
breath. Chachu and his three climbing partners—a Bhutanese
Sherpa, an Indian Army officer, and an Indian climbing
expert—were 23,997 feet above sea level atop a choppy chunk
of ice that was the size of a dining room table and dropped off
thousands of feet on all sides. Attached to each other by a thick
black rope, the men were huddled, football style, with their
arms wrapped around each other's shoulders. Ten hours before
reaching the summit, wearing crampons and heavy down jack-
ets, they had departed Camp III carrying only oxygen tanks,
cans of stewed yak meat, and boiled red rice. The Bhutanese
men had brought small offerings to the deities to leave at the
summit.

Nobody had ever scaled such a tall peak in Bhutan, so this
was a major accomplishment. The climb was even more impressive because the men had not used supplemental oxygen during
the final, backbreaking push from Camp III, which covered
1,500 vertical feet. At the summit, the men weren't especially

fatigued, but they weren't elated either. Buffeted by a vicious Himalayan blizzard, they felt terror that only a mountaineer who's been on a lonely sky-high summit in the midst of a storm can feel.

During this near-death experience, Chachu didn't reminisce about his wife and children or his parents, who were back on the family farm in Dagana, a village in southcentral Bhutan. Nor did Chachu think about his army pals lounging around his base. He was consumed by his immediate experience: the storm, the 50-mile-per-hour winds, the cold, the great distance to safety.

Chachu wasn't sure when he would die, but he was sure it would be soon. Perhaps on his next step he'd slip and free-fall into oblivion. Or, perhaps, death would spare him a few hours and he'd perish during the descent, tripping and falling into a crevasse on the steep route down to Camp III. He was well aware that more than half of all mountaineering deaths occur during the descent.

THIRTY-TWO YEARS LATER, on a balmy, sun-drenched November afternoon, Colonel Chachu (he was promoted after the Jhomolhari expedition) was sipping tea in a rocking chair. He was on the porch outside his wooden house atop a cliff overlooking his little estate 8 miles northeast of Thimphu on the road toward Wangdi. A hundred feet below were Chachu's apple orchards and a gushing river, and the dense woods around the property were full of animals, especially Himalayan black bears.

Inspired by Pema's story about the tragic Jhomolhari expedition and the lone Bhutanese survivor, I launched a minor manhunt after returning to Thimphu to find the survivor, who would turn out to be Chachu. I asked everybody I knew if they had information about what Pema had told me during our trek, but I got nowhere for a couple of weeks. Nobody even knew about the expedition, never mind the one Bhutanese man who survived.

I finally struck gold while giving a golf lesson to Colonel Chimmi at Royal Thimphu. Chimmi is a senior official with the Bhutanese version of the CIA, and his eyes immediately lit up when I asked him about the Jhomolhari tragedy. Not only did he know the whole story, but he also knew the Bhutanese man who had survived and he kindly offered to arrange a meeting with him.

On the morning when we met, Chachu was wearing light blue sweatpants, a pink short-sleeved oxford shirt, a blue fleece jacket, and a thin gray scarf around his neck. He was short and slender— 5'5" and 135 pounds—and he walked with a slight limp.

Chachu spoke only very choppy English, so that morning he spoke in Dzongkha and Chimmi translated between us. When I asked how he got the limp, Chachu said it was from a face-to-face showdown he had with a black bear while he was meandering through his apple orchard. "When the bear attacked I didn't run because those who try to escape will surely die. So I wrestled it," said Chachu in a gentle, mellifluous voice. "I guess I am lucky to have survived."

Surely luck was involved in Chachu's survival, with the bear and on Jhomolhari, but his incredible level of fitness also helped. Chachu told me he was fifty-nine years old, but he looked at least a dozen years younger. He was lithe as a leopard, with not a wrinkle on his tan face, and the muscles on his face and arms were taut and strong.

"I am always fit," said Chachu, who looked hale enough to

climb Jhomolhari that morning. He breathed slowly, with a measured cadence, and he paused before answering each question.

WHEN THE EXPEDITION set out from Paro in early 1970, Chachu had two goals. He wanted to place on the summit a hand-size *bumpa*—a sacred religious relic—that had been given to him by the je khenpo, and he wanted to return to his family alive.

Like most Bhutanese, Chachu was a devout Buddhist. He had not accepted the invitation to scale Jhomolhari because he wanted to climb higher in his kingdom than anybody had ever climbed. "We looked at mountains as gods, which you respect but don't touch. Mountains were never seen as something to be climbed," Chachu said. Rather, the Jhomolhari expedition offered Chachu the chance to commune with deities at one of the most sacred spots in his kingdom and to make the je khenpo and his beloved king proud.

When the four men on the summit decided after a few minutes to begin their descent, they of course didn't know that the events of the next few hours would become one of the most infamous disasters in mountaineering history. At some point shortly after leaving the summit, the Bhutanese Sherpa and one of the Indians would both perish. Chachu has only blurry memories of the deaths. "They fell, yes, but how I do not recall," said Chachu. "My mind was so numb I could not hear or see anything except my footsteps and my breath," said Chachu.

News of the deaths sent shock waves throughout Bhutan that still reverberate. Mountain dwellers feared that the storm was a warning to the people of Bhutan that the mountains were forbidden territory and should be worshipped but never scaled. As word of the disaster spread among mountain dwellers throughout the kingdom, debate among them grew over what they should do to respond. Within a short time, they decided to protest.

Weeks later, a large contingent trekked en masse to Thimphu and marched to demand an audience with government officials. During the meeting, the mountain people made a simple demand: Mountaineering should be banned because otherwise the deities might begin killing innocent people.

The Bhutanese government eventually did what the mountain dwellers requested, and Bhutan became the only country to ban mountaineering. Since then, the ban has remained in place for all but a few short periods, which is remarkable because of the incessant requests that climbers make to open Bhutan's mountains. Indeed, Bhutan not only has scores of desirable peaks to ascend, but it also has the holy grail of mountaineering—the world's tallest unclimbed mountain, the 24,806-foot Gangkar Punsum.

It's no exaggeration to say that hundreds, if not thousands, of mountaineers are chomping at the bit to climb in Bhutan, and especially to attempt Gangkar Punsum. Doug Scott, the British climber who summited 22,274-foot Jichu Drakye in 1988, when Bhutan briefly lifted its ban, told me, "Bhutan has the most prized collection of closed-off mountains in the world, and a lot of expeditions will head for those peaks if the policy changes." Occasionally Bhutan's National Assembly and other government branches debate whether to lift the ban. Those in favor argue that Bhutan could gain enormous tourist income, as Nepal does, but their voices have so far not swayed the majority. "The ban was a reflection of our belief that humans don't have to conquer everything," Ugyen Tshering, Bhutan's minister of communications, told me. "I would not be surprised if the ban is never removed."

CHACHU OFFERED ME a tray of butter cookies, and I took a couple. He then told me about his life.

Chachu was the fifth of nine children in a farming family. At age seventeen he was selected by Jigme Palden Dorji, the late prime minister and Benji's father, to be one of Bhutan's first military officers, and Jigme Palden sent Chachu to an Indian military training center in Kalimpong, in northeastern India. Chachu became an officer, with the rank of second lieutenant, at twenty-one, and he became a major at twenty-nine. Many of his army assignments involved construction, because in the 1960s and 1970s Bhutan was building massive amounts of infrastructure, and two of Chachu's major projects were oversight of the building of the military hospital in Thimphu and the Paro army base.

Chachu had no mountaineering experience before the ascent of Jhomolhari. The idea to attempt the climb had been initiated by Indian Army officers; Bhutanese Army officers agreed to help organize the expedition and supply climbers and support staff. Chachu prepared by jogging, doing exercises indoors, and climbing rocks for a couple of months. "How can you practice for something you've never done?" said Chachu. "We just tried to be physically and mentally fit."

In March 1972, Chachu had been home in Thimphu for a few weeks, his training complete, when he got word that the expedition was to start immediately, so he packed and left. By today's standards, with mountaineers training for up to a year and arriving at base camp weeks, if not months, before the ascent, Chachu and his climbing mates were basically winging it.

The expedition, as Chachu recalled, included seven laborers, one cook, five officers, one climbing instructor from the Darjeeling Mountaineering Institute, and twelve horses. The group walked for three days to reach Haa, a village on the Indian border on the route to Jhomolhari, and after a big *puja*—a religious ceremony officiated by monks—they ventured into the mountains. It took just three days to reach the base camp in Jangothang, where they rested for four days to acclimatize. One of Chachu's few memories of the walk to the base camp was of the food. "We ate the same thing for every meal—rice, ema datse, yak meat, some pork," said Chachu.

One concern Chachu had in the base camp was the lack of navigational maps. "We had nothing," said Chachu.

"So how did you know where to go?" I asked.

"Every day in the base camp, we looked up to see the best way on the mountain," Chachu said. "We tried to determine what would be fast and safe. We decided the best route was to go straight toward the ridge."

From the base camp, Jhomolhari looks a bit like Half Dome, the climbing rock in Yosemite made famous by Ansel Adams's pictures. They're both shaped like an upside-down letter U, the only difference being that Jhomolhari is covered in snow year-round. I recall from our trek to the base camp seeing a couple of ridges on Jhomolhari, but the ridges were all near the summit, and there didn't appear to be any navigable route up the first 95 percent of the mountain.

"For two days, we trekked up and back from base camp, mornings out at four and back by two in the afternoon," Chachu continued. "We did this to set the first base camp, on a small slope, all ice, at nineteen thousand feet. No problem. We did that easily. The weather was so clear."

On the third day, they slept at Camp I and divided into two groups, each with four people, and the groups did two more days of reconnaissance from Camp I. Some men found a huge ice crack on the intended route, so they plotted out another route, from the left side and not the right.

"We set the second camp at twenty-one thousand feet and the third camp at twenty-two thousand four hundred feet," said Chachu, speaking placidly and without emotion.

After several days of reconnaissance, the other group of climbers decided to try for the summit by going up the left side of the upside-down U. But a few climbers got altitude sickness, so the group returned to Camp III. "Their attempt was helpful, though, because they determined that the left side was no good. It has a huge cliff they could not traverse."

A couple of days later, at four o'clock in the morning, Chachu's group left for the summit by heading up the right side of the peak. "There was space just to keep the feet," Chachu recalled. "The trail was so narrow. No other space. Then we reached the top. It was very bad weather. You could see nothing. But we knew it was a steep cliff. That is scary, to know the cliff is there but not see it."

"What did it feel like on the summit?" I asked.

"I was happy, but I could only think I'd never make it back," said Chachu. "I had walked so much and was tired. I had energy only to think of my love for His Majesty and Guru Rinpoche. I remembered, of course, the bumpa. The je khenpo had given it to me. It was small, like my hand, made of bronze and copper. I had good thoughts when I put it on the ice. Then I took the

Bhutanese flag, a small one, and used my ice ax and rope to tie it down. Soon, sometime on the descent, two of the men were gone. Dead. That is all I remember."

Chachu stared pensively at the deep blue sky. He had a look of concern, and this was the first sign of emotion I saw during our two hours together. I could faintly hear the flowing river below. The passing seconds were long and heavy with pain.

"Yes, yes, every day I remember," Chachu said. He paused, then continued. "The feelings of death."

"Do you enjoy talking about the expedition?" I asked.

"I never discuss it because it hurts to talk and nobody cares," said Chachu.

That's not totally true. The Bhutanese and many foreigners interested in Bhutan might not be aware of or interested in the fatal expedition Chachu survived. But most of those people are keenly interested in the fallout from that expedition—the ban on mountaineering—and whether that ban should and will survive. I spoke to some world-renowned climbers about the issue, and I was surprised at how many of them believed that Bhutan should remain closed to mountaineering. "I remember Bhutan as an oasis of sanity," said Doug Scott. "It seemed like the government was really running the country for the benefit of the people rather than the financial gain of individuals. If they open the door to climbing, I'd be surprised if they can find a way to contain it so that it doesn't grow out of control and destroy the culture."

Chapter 15

FROM COKE BOTTLES AND
REBAR TO THE PGA TOUR?

Back at Royal Thimphu, I was watching the kids in
my youth clinic knock around shots and thinking about
Lee Trevino. Like a lot of these kids, Trevino grew up in abject
poverty. He never knew his father and lived in Dallas with his
mother and grandfather, a gravedigger, in a house without electricity and running water. When Trevino was about six, he got
a beat-up club and some balls, began hitting shots in a cow pas-
ture, and was hooked. He taught himself to play and became a
consummate hustler and the winner of twenty-nine PGA Tour
events, including two U.S. Opens, two British Opens, and two
PGA Championships.

But the real reason I was thinking about Trevino was that one
of his hustling tricks was making sucker bets with people who
didn't know him. He would bet that he could hit shots with a
Coke bottle, and the kids in the clinic were teeing off on Royal
Thimphu's first hole, the 100-yard downhill par 3, with Coke
bottles. They were hitting good shots. One little boy, a ten-
year-old caddie, whapped a ball that flew 30 yards and rolled
down the fairway to the front fringe. The kids learned how to

hit balls with bottles for the same reason Trevino did: They couldn't afford golf equipment. When I began teaching a couple of months ago, some of the caddies, all of whom were young boys from poor families, were also playing with bent pieces of rebar. (We have real clubs for the kids now, but they still enjoy playing games with bottles and rebar.)

"These kids could beat most of the adult golfers at Royal Thimphu using Coke bottles and rebar," said Karma Lam Dorji, a 4-handicapper and one of Bhutan's best golfers.

"Imagine how good they'd be if they had real equipment and good coaching." I said.

I invited Karma Lam to the clinic to interview him for a job. So many kids have been attending the youth clinics that Chuck Yash and I conducted most afternoons that we wanted to create a permanent youth golf program here and call it the Bhutan Youth Golf Association (BYGA). When we held clinics at Changlim-ithang, the sports stadium in downtown Thimphu, we often had more than a hundred boys and girls from all socioeconomic backgrounds whacking balls over the crossbars on the soccer goals and into garbage cans. Some of these kids were clearly talented.

Our first task in starting the BYGA was to raise seed money. Chuck solved that problem by offering to let me sell to Bhutanese golfers many of the clubs that Callaway had donated for my teaching, and I raised $3,500. I then told the Royal Thimphu members about the BYGA idea, and they offered to let us use the golf course for clinics. Now we needed to find a Bhutanese who could run the program once Chuck and I left, and Karma Lam was our top candidate.

In his midthirties, Karma Lam had spent a decade overseeing

youth sports programs throughout the kingdom, and he also worked closely with the Bhutanese Olympic Committee. He had helped me conduct the clinic, and was impressive. Having traveled around Europe and Asia for sports management and coaching seminars, he exuded confidence and energy. He also could be strict, which is essential when handling a horde of rambunctious kids. Perhaps best of all, Lyonpo Khandu Wangchuk, the foreign minister and the president of the Bhutan Golf Federation and Royal Thimphu, had given me a glowing endorsement of Karma Lam a few days earlier.

At the end of the clinic I told Karma Lam that we wanted to hire him. I offered to pay him $200 a month and provide all future funding and equipment from the United States. I had no clue how I would raise money for the program in the future, but I figured I'd learn how to fund-raise.

Karma Lam enthusiastically accepted the job, but he had one question: "How will we officially kick off the program?"

Good question. I hadn't thought of that, but I should have, because the Bhutanese love pomp and circumstance, and staging a big event would generate much-needed publicity. As Karma Lam and I sat on the clubhouse steps in the chilly gloaming, I stared up at the mountains and the dark blue, cloudless sky and thought for a minute.

"Here's an idea," I said. "We'll have a junior golf day. We'll get the course for a day and invite every kid in Thimphu to come. We'll have games and contests—"

Karma Lam looked at me like I was crazy. "The only day you could do that would be a Sunday, because the kids are in school every other day," he said. "Good luck getting the members to give up a day of golf for the kids."

"I'll ask Lyonpo Khandu," I said.

"Good luck," said Karma Lam.

I knew it would be impossible to convince the members to give up the course on a Sunday. Like golfers all over the world, the Royal Thimphu members are fiercely protective of their stomping grounds, and for good reason. Many nongolfing Bhutanese think the course should be turned into a recreational area for the public to enjoy. The issue has been raised a few times in the National Assembly, where people have passionately argued that Thimphu's only remaining large swath of green space should not be used for a private club available only to the richest and most powerful people in the kingdom. Luckily for those hundred elite individuals, Royal Thimphu's membership includes many of the country's most prominent leaders (including the king), and the golf course has survived.

Still, I didn't need the members' support. Bhutan would soon be a democracy, but that was not the case then, and to make something happen in Bhutan all you needed was the backing of a very senior official. The best situation was to have the blessing of the king or one of the queens. Next best was the blessing of one of the dozen lyonpos, the highest-ranking government officials. Fortunately, Lyonpo Khandu was not only a golfer, he was also passionate about creating opportunities for kids to play sports, so I had a hunch that he'd use his authority to give me the course to stage a junior golf day.

I was correct. A couple of days after meeting Karma Lam, I saw Lyonpo Khandu at Royal Thimphu, and he approved my idea on the spot, and the course was ours for an upcoming Sunday.

I KNOCKED ON Khandu-Om's door at six-thirty A.M. Silence. I knocked again. I heard a sleepy woman's voice. "Okay, okay," Khandu-Om said. "I'll be ready in five minutes."

Khandu-Om was one of Tobgye's two daughters. In 2001 she graduated from The College of Wooster, in Ohio, where she played on the basketball team, and since returning to Bhutan she had worked at UNICEF and lived in the little cottage on the hillside between our house and her parents' house. Khandu-Om was a good golfer, and she volunteered to work at the junior golf day.

When we arrived at the course at seven, nobody else was around, unless you counted the cows grazing in the tall fescue down by the fifth fairway.

"How many people are you expecting?" asked Khandu-Om.

"Between twenty-five and five hundred," I said.

I was only half joking. During the past week I had become a one-man publicity machine on behalf of the junior golf day. I guessed that some of the hundred kids who were attending my daily clinics would come, but I wanted a few hundred kids to attend, and to get that many, I knew I had to pound the pavement. So I designed a flyer, printed a thousand copies, and spent a few hours every day walking around town telling people about the event and posting flyers in stores. I also placed an advertisement in *Kuensel*.

I figured that golf wasn't enough of a hook to convince most Bhutanese to attend, because most of them didn't know anything about the game. So I focused my sales pitch on three things: Lyonpo Khandu had endorsed the event; it was going to be like a carnival with games, contests, food, and prizes; and everything was free. Lots of adults said they'd come and bring their kids, but I was still nervous. I felt like my reputation was riding on the success of the day.

By seven-thirty, the eight adults who'd volunteered to help had arrived. We set up two reception tables on the grass in front of the clubhouse, where children would register and get their free Callaway golf hats, and we set up different games around the course. The second hole had a long-driving contest; the third green had putting; the eighth hole had a closest-to-the-pin game; and the practice bunker and green by the clubhouse had a short-game contest.

At eight o'clock I gathered the volunteers to give them final directions for the day. "This will either be a total failure," I said, "or it'll be like *Field of Dreams* and kids will just appear out of nowhere."

AT ABOUT EIGHT-THIRTY, children started to trickle in. An eight-year-old girl, Chukki, said she had walked twenty minutes to come at her parents' urging, and there was a mother and father with three young children in tow. By eight forty-five the trickle of guests had become a torrent. Dozens of children were surrounding the registration tables and clamoring for free hats.

"Holy cow," Chuck said. "I think we've got a monster on our hands."

By nine o'clock there were at least three hundred people at Royal Thimphu, almost all of them kids. I knew the club had never seen anything like this.

"It's a good thing most of the members aren't here," said Palden Tshering, laughing. "They'd freak out because they'd be afraid the course will get destroyed."

I had the same thought, except I was laughing inside. "That's why I recruited volunteers like you," I said. "You guys have to keep the kids in order."

I stood on the front steps to officially greet the sea of ebullient little kids, almost all of them wearing ghos and kiras. The volunteers stood behind me. The sight was overwhelming. This was going to work. Golf might have a real future in Bhutan.

We divided the kids into groups of twenty-five, balancing them with a mix of ages (which ranged from four to eighteen), genders (one hundred of the three hundred kids were girls), and abilities. The plan was for each group to spend thirty minutes at each of the half dozen games we had arranged, and that worked for a while.

The problem was the little concrete pond in front of the first green. The first group of the day on this hole had a few kids who hit their balls into the pond, and a few of the caddies promptly stripped naked and jumped into the pond to retrieve the balls. The water was waist deep, so the caddies easily retrieved the balls by feeling around for them with their feet, but after tossing them back to the group, the caddies remained in the water to play. Soon other kids in the group undressed and jumped in to join the splashing and diving, and it wasn't long before kids from around the course began running to the pond to join the fun. Fortunately, the adult volunteers were able to corral the kids back to their groups, and each group stayed together, more or less, for the morning.

By noon the groups had completed their circuits of the games set up on the course, and the droves of kids were all milling around the first fairway while dozens of kids were playing in the pond by the green. I wasn't sure whether the situation was out of control, but there was too much innocent yelling and laughing for me to quash the games. Instead, I ordered the volunteers to keep the kids off the first green and out of the bunker, and prayed that the fairway wouldn't be trampled too badly.

At twelve-thirty, we told the kids that lunch was ready, and they stampeded up to the clubhouse for white rice, ema datse, mo mos, steamed vegetables, and cake. For most of these kids, a free lunch at Royal Thimphu was an unfathomable treat.

"I think we hit gold," said Chuck, as Carrie and I stood alongside him in front of the clubhouse.

Perhaps we had hit gold, but only time would tell. In my dreams, I'd return to Bhutan in twenty years to find kids all over the kingdom playing at courses that had been carved out of wide-open farmland. Most of the kids would be playing for fun, but some would be serious competitors. There'd also be some Bhutanese competing on professional tours around the world, including the PGA Tour.

Was that just wishful thinking? Going from Bhutan to the tour would not be the most unlikely route to golfing riches ever taken. Vijay Singh grew up dirt poor whacking balls in Fiji, which might be more remote than Bhutan. Remember, Bhutan is next to India, and India has a burgeoning golf craze and a banner crop of young and successful tour professionals. So any Bhutanese youngsters who excel would have to go only as far as their neighbor India to hone their games and compete at a high level. Vijay Singh had to travel thousands of miles to take his game from a ratty driving range to the pro ranks.

But, I thought, just getting kids to play golf in Bhutan might be a big problem because there was just one nine-hole course for them to use, and the members at Royal Thimphu were highly protective of their turf. Still, I was optimistic. "Who knows? We might have the next Tiger Woods in Bhutan," Randy told me during a lesson. "He could be one of the kids in your clinics, or he might be some boy out in a remote part of the kingdom. Anything's possible, right?"

Chapter 16

AN ISLAND UNTO HIMSELF:
BHUTAN'S ONLY PRIEST

KARMA LAM DIDN'T accept the job of running the BYGA for the money. He was part of an affluent family—their businesses included soft-drink bottling and trading with Tibetans—that had connections to the Bhutanese royals, and he lived in his family's gated compound on the eastern side of Thimphu. The compound had two large modern houses and an apartment above a garage, and Karma Lam, married with a young son, and his five siblings lived there with their families and their mother. The compound had a few very small lawns that were dotted with apple trees and gardens containing bougainvillea and pink and red roses. The capacious driveway was full of vehicles—a Land Cruiser and a Hyundai SUV, for example—that would be middle-class rides in America but are affordable only to the wealthy in Bhutan.

One morning, Karma Lam and I were in the compound. We were sitting at a table beneath a big lawn umbrella next to an apple tree from which Lam plucked a few red apples for us to eat while we drank tea. The views were dramatically mixed. Look up and you saw the forested mountains rising vertically to the ocean-blue sky. Look straight ahead and you saw a wall that was built to hide the ugly commercial sprawl around the compound— a gas station, some auto repair shops, and a cluster of industrial buildings that included the editorial offices and a printing plant for *Kuensel*.

Lam and I discussed plans for how the BYGA would operate after I returned to New York, and then he took me into one of the houses. We entered through sliding glass doors into one of the most sleek and lavishly decorated living rooms I had seen in Bhutan. Everything was new, and I felt like I was in a New York City condo. There were white leather couches, a large black glass coffee table, pinewood bookcases, waist-high Chinese vases with silk flowers, and a lacquer table from Burma. But not everything felt like it was from outside of Bhutan. The tables and bookcases had framed snapshots from family gatherings, showing people in ghos and kiras with solemn faces and their arms hanging down at their sides. This was not unusual. For some reason, Bhutanese rarely hug and smile for family portraits.

One picture caught my eye. It showed a tall, fit Bhutanese man in a priest's uniform—black shirt, white collar, a metal cross hanging around his neck.

"Who is *that*?" I asked.

"He's my brother, Father Kinley [pronounced "kin-*lay*"]," Karma Lam said. "The only Bhutanese who's ever been an ordained priest."

It seemed like an impossible oxymoron: a Bhutanese priest. But Karma Lam insisted it was genuine. "You really have to meet Father Kinley. He's my hero and role model. Maybe the greatest Bhutanese alive, save for His Majesty."

"Where is he? How can I meet him?" I said.

Karma Lam grew quiet, pensive. He glanced outside through

the sliding glass doors. "Father Kinley cannot live in Bhutan. It would not work," he said.

The silence was uncomfortable. I had never seen Karma Lam so emotional.

"Why?" I asked.

"In Bhutan, my brother is a ghost. Hardly anybody knows about him, and many of those who do know think he's a traitor," said Karma Lam, measuring each word. "He is in India. He is the rector and principal at North Point, the boarding school in Darjeeling. When he comes to visit, you must meet him."

ON ANOTHER SUNNY morning, I was back in the living room sitting on one of the leather sofas and talking to Karma Lam and his older sister, Dechen. Father Kinley (his full Bhutanese name is Kinley Tshering) was to return to Bhutan a few days later to see his relatives, and I was there to learn as much about the mysterious man as I could before meeting him.

Raised in a devoutly Buddhist famly, Kinley was a precocious, intense tyke. But the horoscope the monks gave him when he was born on December 24, 1958, said he might die as a child, and Kinley's parents, like many Bhutanese, deeply believed the veracity of the horoscopes, so to save him from that fate his parents enrolled him in the monkhood at age four. His parents believed that turning their son over to the monkhood would gain them and Kinley merit and appease the gods, and that those things would perhaps be able to reverse Kinley's fortunes. "I can still picture him in his red monk robe and red scarf," said Dechen. "So cute!"

After around one year, though, Kinley's parents felt that his evil spirits had been purged, so they withdrew him from the monkhood and sent him, along with his siblings, to a Catholic boarding school in Darjeeling, India. Kinley studied in Darjeeling from kindergarten through high school and then went to a junior college in Bangalore for two years. After that he spent a couple of years at St. Xavier's College in Mumbai, where he received a bachelor's degree in sociology, and he earned an MBA from the Indian Institute of Management Bangalore (IIMB), one of the best business schools in the world. (Every year, 175,000 people apply for 250 places at IIMB.) When he was twenty-three years old Kinley returned to Bhutan from India to run the family soft-drink bottling business in Phuentsholing for three years. But while there he discovered that he wasn't very happy as a businessman, although his leadership helped the soft-drink company thrive. Rather, Kinley found that he had one true passion—Christianity—and he wanted to become a priest.

At age twenty-six, Kinley resigned from the soft-drink business and set out on the path to priesthood by formally joining the Jesuits. He studied as a Jesuit for several years in India and the United States, and was finally ordained as a priest at age thirty-six on October 23, 1995.

As a priest Father Kinley decided to devote his working life to education, and his first job was as a schoolteacher at a prep school in northeastern India. He also became an indefatigable humanitarian, a "Bhutanese Gandhi," said Karma Lam. Father Kinley has been honored throughout India for his community service, most of which is directed toward underprivileged children. His charitable works have included the creation of programs to provide free healthcare, meals, and educational scholarships to poor children. Most recently, Father Kinley started a program at North Point that turns the school into a sanctuary for seven hundred poor children during school holidays by having the kids sleep in the school's dorms, eat meals in the cafeterias, and receive counseling from the school's teachers and administrators.

Karma Lam and Dechen spoke as reverently about Kinley as most Bhutanese do about His Majesty, and they often teared up during our chat. They told how when Kinley was a boy his own parents shunned him, and other parents used to try to not let their children play with Kinley because they were afraid he was a devil. But Karma Lam, Dechen, and their siblings never wavered in their support of Kinley's religious devotion because they felt it was preordained. "Brother was born on Christmas Eve, and things like that always made me at peace because they show that Kinley is where God wants him to be," said Dechen.

I'm sure there was some hero-worshipping in the effusive praise Karma Lam and his sister were heaping upon their brother. But to provide evidence of Father Kinley's good works, Karma Lam showed me some Indian newspaper articles about humanitarian awards Father Kinley had received. He also showed me the yearbook from North Point, the school Father Kinley now runs, and it included a glowing biography.

"Did you know other Bhutanese who were Christians?" I asked.

"No, which is why my parents thought it was all wrong," said Dechen. "In Bhutan, we have such strong religious attachment to Buddhism, so even with all the kids who went out to India to school, nobody converted to Christianity. My parents used to ask about Kinley and his praying at school, but I always told them it was nothing to worry about. Then in class ten Kinley shocked me by saying he wanted to get baptized."

"Did your parents ever accept Kinley's Christian faith?" I asked.

"Eventually Mom kind of got over it, but not Dad," said

Karma Lam. "When Kinley had his ordination ceremony at the school where he taught in India, Dad was the only person from the family who refused to attend. It's too bad, because it was the most beautiful day. Sunny, thousands of people packed into the school courtyard, Father Kinley leading a Mass, guest speakers telling about his charitable works. I was in tears. The ironic thing is that Dad died on Christmas Day, in 2000. So perhaps Dad was saying something."

News of the ordination didn't make a blip on the radar in Bhutan. *Kuensel* didn't mention it, and nobody talked about it. Not positively, anyway.

In Bhutan, the persecution that Father Kinley endured included primarily verbal taunts said directly to him or behind his back. He was also ostracized socially, and often found himself not being invited to dinners and weddings. That some of the most severe taunting came directly from Father Kinley's parents, especially his father, was hurtful to Father Kinley and his siblings.

"People just couldn't fathom it," said Karma Lam. "To me, it was a sad day because it felt like we, as a family and a nation, were losing one of our great leaders, and that still hurts."

Dechen's eyes were moist. "I console myself by knowing that Kinley is happy," she said. "He had to go through so much, so I know this is what he wants. When studying for the priesthood in India, he used to stay alone in meditation for six months, and Mother and I would go visit. We'd get a special permit to see him for a half hour. He was just skin and bones. We would give Kinley gifts—rice cookers, biscuits, cheese, cash—but I know he gave it all away to more needy people."

"Kinley overcame the desire for wants," said Karma Lam. "He lives to give."

Karma Lam rose, walked over to the picture of his brother,

and intently stared at it. "Someday our nation will pay tribute to this amazing man," said Karma Lam. "Not in this lifetime. But someday."

Perhaps it won't be as long as Karma Lam thinks. The chief justice told me that once democracy takes root he thinks it will be inevitable that churches for faiths other than Buddhism and Hinduism will be built in Bhutan, probably in his lifetime. If a Catholic worship hall is built in Bhutan, it would be hard to imagine a more ideal candidate than Father Kinley to deliver the first sermon.

"MAYBE YOU CAN teach me to play golf," said Father Kinley. "I'm terrible."

"I've caddied for priests," I said. "But I've never given a priest a lesson."

"Maybe you should keep it like that," Father Kinley said with a chuckle. "I might ruin your career."

Father Kinley and I were in the same living room where his brother and sister told me about him. We were sitting on white leather couches across from each other. He was wearing blue jeans, a white T-shirt, a blue fleece pullover with long sleeves, and black leather loafers.

"You don't wear your collar in Bhutan?" I asked.

"Why would I do that?" said Father Kinley.

Good point. That would be asking for trouble.

But Father Kinley wasn't concerned about attracting attention. "I don't wear the collar often at home. I usually wear stuff like this or a gho. I'm Bhutanese, right?"

I thought about a story Karma Lam had told me. When Father Kinley was running the family bottling business in southern

Bhutan, he unofficially adopted a young Bhutanese man of Nepalese descent who had indigent parents. Doing that was essentially heretical: bluebloods like Kinley's family often look down on those with Nepalese blood as second-class citizens. "Taking the boy under his wing was a very bold move," said Karma Lam.

Father Kinley let the young man move into his house and urged him to become a pilot. He sent him to train with the Indian Air Force and then arranged and paid for him to attend college. The young man was set to become a pilot for Druk Air, but at the last minute the government quashed his dream. "The government wouldn't let him fly," said Father Kinley. "They made some excuses about the political furor over the Nepali refugee situation in the south, so I understood the hesitation Druk Air had to let him fly."

Father Kinley was being diplomatic; one person told me the real reason why they clipped his wings "was because of his Nepali blood."

"I've been called everything: hero, rebel, traitor, and martyr, to name a few," said Father Kinley, laughing. Once, at a wedding in Bhutan, a little boy approached Father Kinley and said, "You're a strange man." When Father Kinley asked the boy why he had said that, he replied, "My mother told me you're a madman."

"That was very funny," said Father Kinley. "I understand that some parents think I will try to influence their children, so they want to keep me away."

It's hard to tell what's behind Father Kinley's laughter. Did he really forgive the hatred and racism heaped upon him by his countrymates? Or did he laugh as a way of deflecting deep feelings of rejection and sadness?

"By and large, the Bhutanese have been good to me about my Christianity," Father Kinley said. "Individuals here and there have made caustic remarks and made me feel like a second-class citizen. You know, not inviting me to a dinner or a wedding, and not acknowledging my presence in a social setting. But in general, the people have been tolerant."

"What do you consider yourself?" I asked.

"I'm just a human being on a journey searching for the meaning of life. I won't categorize myself or anybody else; that is never helpful. As a young boy, I realized that standing alone can be painful and lonely, but it can also be joyful."

The young Kinley worked in the family store, hauling bags of rice to earn spending money, and he would frequently jog alone around Thimphu and on the paths that wind through the surrounding forests. "I'd go for maybe twelve miles," Father Kinley said. "My favorite part was going along the river. I'm on a journey, and that river is continuously moving, too. It gives you the sense of Buddhist impermanence. I love that."

Father Kinley had happy memories of growing up in a devoutly Buddhist home. He especially enjoyed the rituals involved with visiting monasteries. He said, "I fondly recall our family outings to pay homage to local deities. We'd light butter lamps, prostrate, burn juniper, watch the mask dances during the tsechu for a few days."

Father Kinley first learned about Christianity when he was seven or eight years old. He was out of the monkhood and living in Bhutan, and his siblings' friends from boarding school used to send Christmas cards to Bhutan. "They had very religious images of Mary, Joseph, and the baby Jesus. We'd never seen anything like that. I'd never even heard of Jesus," said Father Kinley. "But the cards resonated. I was fascinated with the little child in the pictures."

When Father Kinley went off to the Catholic school in India, he made the connection between the cards and what he saw around the school. "The first time I went to Catholic church at school, my small mind began to attach the small baby on the Christmas cards to the man dying on the crosses I saw all over the church," Father Kinley said. "I was curious what happened to this man that made people kill him. Questions like that filled my mind."

Father Kinley continued, "I recall one glorious afternoon entering the Bethany School chapel. Sunlight was filtering through the stained glass and this beautiful glint of light was shining on a big wooden cross. I felt drawn to the wonder of this illumination and the beautiful man, all in brass, on the cross. I was alone that afternoon and the golden hue shines in my mind now."

Christianity percolated in Father Kinley's mind for eight years. Finally, at age fifteen, when he was a student at a Jesuit school in India called St. Joseph's, "I just got this strong impulse that I had to commit myself to Christianity and get baptized," Father Kinley continued. "I felt that I had to choose between Buddhism and Christianity. I went to my rector, Father Gerard, and he completely dissuaded me. 'There's no need to become a Christian,' he said. 'Just be a good person and enjoy your life. When you're twenty-one, you can decide.'"

Father Kinley was deeply disappointed. He'd expected the father would welcome his eagerness to be baptized. During a school holiday, he returned to the family's house in Phuentsholing, in southern Bhutan, and the town had a Don Bosco technical school run by Salesian fathers from Italy. He went to the school, and its director, Father Phillip Geraldo, agreed to baptize him. Over the next few weeks in Bhutan, Father Kinley didn't tell anybody what he'd done. The first person he told about the baptism was Father Gerard, back at his school.

Father Gerard was so displeased that the young Kinley had disobeyed him that he convened a special meeting of the school's priests to decide whether he should be expelled. "They decided, barely, to keep me in school," said Father Kinley.

Father Kinley kept his secret from everybody in Bhutan for a full year, and then he broke the news to his parents.

"My mother was kind of okay with the news, but my father was mad and upset," recalled Father Kinley. "He scolded me. He shouted, 'You're not loyal or faithful! I looked after you all these years and you betrayed me!' "

A few days later, some soldiers came to Father Kinley's house. They told the teenager that His Majesty had requested an audience and that they would return at eight o'clock the following morning to pick him up. Father Kinley asked what His Majesty wanted to discuss, but the soldiers claimed they didn't know. "I was just testing them," said Father Kinley. "I knew well why the king had requested to see me."

Somehow, Father Kinley slept peacefully that night. "I was so convinced of what I'd done that after the soldiers left and I pondered the situation, my fear dissipated," said Father Kinley. "This thought from the Bible gave me courage: 'When you go before princes and kings, don't worry what you have to say. My spirit will speak to you.' "

The next morning, Father Kinley wore a gho and a white scarf—which common Bhutanese are compelled to wear in the presence of a dignitary—and the soldiers drove him to the palace in a jeep. As he sat waiting in a vestibule, Father Kinley thought about how young His Majesty was, only nineteen years old, and that comforted him. He felt like he'd be talking to somebody on his wavelength. After half an hour, the soldiers led Father Kinley back to the king's chambers. The soldiers left, and Father Kinley bowed. The king, sitting on a throne, was silent. He stared, emotionless, at Father Kinley for what seemed an eternity. "Let's go for a walk," the king said, and he then led Father Kinley out to a garden where he pointed out his collection of animals, which included a leopard, a bear, and dogs, all of them in cages.

The king went silent again and fed the animals. "I was feeling very strange. There were no words," said Father Kinley.

Then His Majesty went inside, and Father Kinley waited out in the garden. The king hadn't asked him to come inside, and it was not proper to go anyplace unless the king gave directions. After standing amid the garden and animals for five minutes, a soldier came out and led Father Kinley back into the chambers. The king asked father Kinley to sit across from him on the floor.

"Why did you become a Christian?" said the king.

"I find peace and confidence in Jesus," Father Kinley replied.

"You don't find that in Buddhism?' asked the king.

Father Kinley chuckled at this point in the story. He said, "In my naïve style, I was so nervous, I just blurted, 'No.' "

The king replied with a little smile. "Then I knew everything was okay," said Father Kinley. "He was very gracious. He said he had no problem for me to be a Christian. He asked just that I be a good Bhutanese."

Next, the king abruptly changed the topic of discussion, asking Father Kinley what sports he played and where he'd like to study. Right there, the king called his minister of development, who was waiting outside the chambers. When the dasho entered, the king said, "Give him a scholarship anywhere he asks to go."

The king then dismissed Father Kinley, and Dasho Lam led him out of the chambers. "I was so happy," said Father Kinley. "His Majesty could have put me in prison and said, 'We're Buddhists and you're finished.'"

I wondered, though: By offering to send Father Kinley abroad, was the king trying to get him out of Bhutan? Probably not. The king knew that there was no place in Bhutan for a Catholic priest to work, and it was common for the king to have the government provide scholarships to study abroad for children of high-ranking officials and other promising youngsters so they could later fill key government jobs.

Father Kinley rose from the couch and stretched his arms. He led me upstairs to the family's prayer room, a small square space that was filled with an odor from burning incense. For a couple of moments, Father Kinley and I stood in rich silence, our heads bowed and eyes closed. Then a small, elderly woman in a colorful kira tiptoed through the open door. Father Kinley turned and smiled softly, but he didn't move. "That's Mother," he whispered to me. The elegant woman walked to his right side, paused, and then bent down so her knees, toes, and forehead touched the floor. The woman softly chanted prayers in Dzongkha, and the gentle reverberations of the words were peaceful but invigorating.

As Father Kinley's mother continued praying and prostrating, he spoke. "I call myself a Buddhist-Christian," he said. "The Vatican might throw me out if they hear that, but I've always felt that I was just putting a Christian coat over my Buddhist shirt. Many Christian converts renounce everything in their past. But my views of religion in thirty years have come full circle. I don't reject anything of Buddhist philosophy. The way I meditate and contemplate is very Buddhist. I have taken a thirty-year journey, and I think I am more universal through it all. Mankind needs much more interreligious dialogue because religion is not supposed to separate, but bring people together."

Father Kinley then discussed the future of Christianity in Bhutan. He was cautiously optimistic that the kingdom's new democracy would be a boon not only for Christians but for people of all faiths. "It's the dawn of a new beginning, and I'm hopeful that all people will now be able to freely exercise their personal beliefs without suffering," he said. "But I am worried about fundamentalists. They might come in and try to take advantage of this situation by proselytizing. That would be very unfortunate."

"Do you wish you could be a priest in Bhutan?" I asked.

Father Kinley had no regrets. He smiled and replied, "I am just happy to have my special niche as a Bhutanese Christian."

Chapter 17

WANT TO SPEAK TO THE KING?
JUST LOOK HIM UP
IN THE PHONE BOOK

FOR ME, THE most amazing thing about Bhutan is its phone book. Bhutan Telecom publishes a single 262-page tome that includes every number in the kingdom. Yes, *every* number for *everyone*. Forget unlisted numbers, secret numbers, or numbers you need a special code to dial. Bhutan could be the only place on earth where you can let your fingers do the walking to reach *anybody*.

Want to call the king? There he is, on the unique aqua blue page at the beginning of the book that has numbers for everybody in the royal family. You can reach the king at his office in the Thimphu dzong at 322521 (don't forget to add 975 for the country code and 2 for the Thimphu city code) or at his palace, Samtenling, at 322835. If he doesn't pick up, you can call the palace pantry, 323168.

No luck? Maybe His Majesty went to Punakha, a village 50 miles east of Thimphu, near Wangdi, where the boss has a winter getaway palace. His number in Punakha is 584193 (the city code is also 2). He spends time in Punakha in the winter because

Punakha is only 4,100 feet above sea level—3,400 feet lower than Thimphu—so the weather is much more temperate. The king also has a little nine-hole golf course on his property across the river from the stunning and massive Punakha dzong, which was completely renovated a few years ago and sits on a spit of land between the confluence of two roaring rivers. When he plays golf—and he rarely plays anymore because he's so busy with the kingdom's shift to democracy—he plays holes at his own layout on his own property in Punakha.

Want to reach the chief justice to arrange a get-together to discuss gross national happiness? I did, so I turned to page 107 in the phone book and dialed the chief justice's office. His personal assistant, a friendly woman named Sonam, answered and set up an appointment for me.

I'm not sure if she would do the same for a stranger. But I wouldn't be surprised. Bhutan Telecom doesn't list everybody's number by accident. They know about security and privacy. But they also know that one of the big reasons Bhutan is so peaceful and happy—no, it's not nirvana, but it's the happiest place I've ever been—is the strong sense of humility, openness, and compassion that pervades every aspect of the culture. Those ideals trickle down from the top. Indeed, the king spends considerable time throughout the year among the people, walking through towns and trekking in remote areas of the kingdom to talk with hoi polloi and stay in touch with day-to-day life. Bhutanese also have the right to appeal any legal ruling, from a parking ticket to murder, to the king and he never turns down legitimate requests for one-on-one meetings with citizens in such cases.

A FEW DAYS after I set up my meeting with the chief justice, at about three P.M., I was sitting on the steps in front of the High Court. There were about fifteen steps, each a foot wide and thirty feet long, in front of the imposing structure. Ahead of me was the 100-yard driveway that led uphill from the public road to the court. The driveway had two lanes, separated by a median planted with flowers and bushes. On each side of the driveway there was a row of medium-height pine trees. The sight reminded me of Magnolia Drive in Augusta, the most famous road in golf, which is about the same length as the road into the High Court, and also has two lanes and is surrounded by about sixty majestic magnolia trees on each side.

It was so quiet out there, and I was all alone. Nobody was coming or going. I was excited but not nervous. This wasn't my first meeting with the chief justice, and Carrie had been working with him for a while on the new evidence act and penal code.

Sonam tapped me on the back.

"Chief is ready," she said.

Sonam led me through the lobby, which, like the rest of the building, is made of very old wood, and led me up some creaky stairs to the second floor. Sonam knocked on a door and the chief justice opened it.

What a smile. It was as radiant, cheerful, and sincere as Benji's. He escorted me to a corner of his chambers where there were some chodrums.

We started out with small talk. He wanted to know how we liked Bhutan and how Claudia was adjusting. Then I asked for a little personal history. Funny, he loved McDonald's (Big Macs were his favorite American food), and his favorite business suits were the ones he had bought at Barneys during a visit to New York several years earlier.

We then discussed gross national happiness. The chief justice leaned forward for emphasis. "The amazing thing about our king is his vision," he said. "He never speaks off the cuff, but when he first uttered 'gross national happiness,' nobody appreciated what he was saying. We didn't even appreciate it until it became a big issue."

"What's the real purpose of GNH?" I asked.

"I hope it will provide freedom and enjoyment for our kingdom. Everybody wants happiness, but few really have it. Indeed, happiness kills. By that, I mean depression is a big killer, and if there is such a disease it is our duty to seek medicine as a remedy. That medicine, for us, is gross national happiness."

"What are the roots of GNH?" I asked.

"It is everywhere in the world," the chief justice replied. "Look no further than your forefathers, who in their Declaration of Independence said that among the unalienable rights given by our creator are 'life, liberty, and the pursuit of happiness.'"

Uh, well, of course. I felt pretty stupid. How had I not thought of that? It seems like back home we Americans have forgotten about pursuing happiness, unless you count pursuing money and houses and cars as sources of happiness.

The chief justice continued, "The goal must be to reach all citizens, but we cannot expect to have all of our people happy. But I do expect to see most of them smiling. That cannot come, though, unless we continue thinking, meditating, and working. These are my wishful dreams."

LARGE BUT ORDINARY. That was my first impression of the chief justice's house as we pulled into his driveway a week after my meeting with him at the High Court. Instead of the palace I'd expected, it was a two-floor concrete house in a residential neighborhood, wedged into a modest lot ringed by a concrete wall. Inside, the décor was ordinary, too. There were simple wood and leather sofas, chairs and tables, and a few artifacts and pictures on the walls.

What was not ordinary, though, were the books. There were thousands of them, crammed onto the shelves in the living room, dining room, and den. I had never seen so many books in a house in Bhutan, and the variety of the volumes was as impressive as the number, a testament to the chief justice's insatiable appetite for knowledge. I saw copies of *The Elements of Style*, Shakespeare's plays, Tibetan-English dictionaries, biographies of John Adams and Thomas Jefferson.

"What's the one book you don't have that you really want?" I asked the chief justice.

"Muhammad Ali," he said with his impish grin. "I want to know about this fascinating man and his downfall, how he lost his fortune."

The chief justice led us into the den and we sat down. Two other justices from the High Court sat around us.

I noticed some silver swords hanging on a wall. "You're not a hunter, are you?" I said.

The chief justice chuckled. "No, but these swords have all been used in battle," he said. The chief justice was wearing a sword, held in a silver sheath tied to the waist belt around his gho. Before coming to Bhutan, I surely would have been a little unnerved seeing a dinner companion prepared for hand-to-hand combat, but now it was routine. High-ranking officials, including the chief justice, always wore swords to formal meetings and social affairs, so I was only curious to hear the history of the chief justice's blades.

"Look at the marks," he said, pulling the sword from its case. There were little nicks along the sharp side of the blade. "Each nick is for a kill," he said.

"A *what?*"

"Some of these swords were used in real battles, and some were used to hunt," the chief justice said.

I switched subjects. "It's hard to imagine that you and Benji are the pillars of the judicial system," I said.

Chuckles all around. On the surface, the chief justice and Benji, who was the first chief justice, seemed like polar opposites. Benji was a nonstop party animal who used to be a great athlete. The chief justice was jocular but reserved and likely has not been to a bar—or a gym—for a very long time. But both were deep thinkers, tireless workers, history buffs, and passionately devoted to their homeland. Also, each shared a keen sense of global politics and deep mutual respect.

"Benji. What a wonderful man who has done so much for Bhutan," said the chief justice. "Just watch out for his stories."

"Are they all true?" Carrie asked.

"You'd be surprised," the chief justice said. "They all are at least based in truth, even if there is some exaggeration."

The chief justice led the conversation into the dining room, where a beautiful buffet was set up, with elegant china laden with ema datse, fried chicken, ground beef that reminded me of Hamburger Helper, red and white rice, steamed vegetables, and some fiery chili paste, which Carrie loved.

Back in the living room, we sat down and ate while holding plates on our laps. I wondered: Are justices on the U.S. Supreme Court so casual and cheerful? Do they, like their Bhutanese counterparts, enjoy an occasional whiskey?

During dinner, Carrie and the chief justice fell into passionate discussion of their work. There was an obvious affection there; this had been the most exhilarating job of Carrie's life, and the chief justice had graciously shepherded her through the experience.

"What have you learned from your work?" the chief justice asked.

Carrie paused. She was on the spot now. I was a little nervous, too.

"When I was starting, you told me about the crest of the High Court, the golden yoke wrapped in a silken knot," Carrie replied. "You said it was a symbol of secular law, and that the knot was essential, because it can be loosened to remind the court to temper punishment with compassion. But it can also be tightened to remind the court that sometimes the severity of the crime warrants less compassion. I've learned how hard but important it is to find that ideal balance in my work, especially the penal code."

The chief justice, arms folded over his lap, smiled. He seemed very pleased. He then quoted Oliver Wendell Holmes, Jr., a United States Supreme Court justice from 1902 to 1932, as having said, "We live by symbols because symbols inspire us."

"Your work seems much inspired by our treasured High Court crest, and I am deeply grateful for your devotion," the chief justice said.

Carrie returned a smile as beaming as I'd ever seen on her face. "Thank you, Chief Justice," she said meekly with a little bow of her head.

The discussion then turned to the crime situation in Bhutan. Bhutan is still far from a litigious country, and crime is rare. But crime is increasing as the kingdom modernizes, so the chief justice is spearheading the development of a twenty-first-century judicial system. In most crimes and disputes, local officials still mediate settlements and punishments. If they can't settle a dispute, it is likely handled in the court system, which has four levels: trial courts, an appeals court, the High Court, and finally the king, to whom anybody can take a final appeal. The courts, which have branches and judges spread throughout the kingdom, have no juries. Instead, judges decide on everything from guilt and innocence to damages, sentences, and restitution. The courts typically conduct investigations, although prosecutors recently have been introduced to the system. Most defendants represent themselves, but those who can afford it hire as defense counsel what somebody from the West would consider a paralegal.

Court trials are rare, but a few weeks prior there had been a monumental trial in Thimphu. It involved a gold smuggling case that was the first example of major organized crime in Bhutan, to some an omen that modernization might destroy the kingdom. Bhutanese authorities uncovered a massive ring in which about fifty people, including businessmen and every customs official at the Paro airport, were allegedly working with a large Asian smuggling operation and using Bhutan as a hub in the network that illegally trafficked gold throughout Asia. During her first day attending the trial in Thimphu, Carrie was stunned to see a couple of Royal Thimphu members among the defendants. "We locked eyes and it was bizarre," said Carrie. The two men were people she'd played golf with and I'd taught. The trial lasted for twenty-eight days, and one of the members was among the forty-seven people convicted and sent to prison, with sentences ranging from three to eight years; the other member was acquitted.

At dinner, Carrie and the chief justice discussed the new

Bhutanese constitution and its origins. The chief justice had read constitutions from dozens of countries to prepare for drafting Bhutan's new charter. The chief justice said the shortest he had read were from Bahrain and Sweden; both, he said, were less than twenty pages. "Perhaps that is too short, at least for us," he said. "Ours will be around forty pages."

"Why are you going ahead with a constitution?" said Carrie. "It seems like many people prefer to just stick with the king."

"It will take time, but the people will see that His Majesty is doing everything for the future happiness and peace of our kingdom," the chief justice said. "Change is never easy."

"I agree," said Sherpa, one of the other justices. "People often do not agree with the vision of a leader, especially when the vision is so radically different from the status quo."

The chief justice, perhaps tired of nation-building (or perhaps just to make me feel at home), changed the topic. "Why is Tiger Woods so good?" he asked.

"His mind," I replied. "Tiger thinks, plans, and organizes better than anybody."

"I like that," the chief justice said. "We need more thinkers."

"Do our young golfers have potential?" asked Sherpa.

We hadn't spoken about golf that night, but the justices clearly knew about the work I'd been doing with the children.

"Yes, but the children need a chance to compete," I said. "I see the same raw talent in your children as I see in juniors in America. But your kids will have to fight like warriors if they want to become professionals, because they have so few resources. Still, it's possible to succeed. Do you know Vijay Singh?"

"Yes, yes," said the chief justice.

"He was poor while growing up in Fiji," I said. "He left as a teenager with big dreams of becoming rich and famous, and after more than a decade of toiling in poverty he began to succeed. Now he's a multimillionaire and major champion."

"What is your history?" Carrie asked the chief justice.

"Me?" he said. "Why do you care about somebody so trivial?"

"Nobody is trivial," I said.

"You sound like a Buddhist," the chief justice said.

"What will Bhutan be like in fifty years?" I asked.

The chief justice laughed. "That is a beautiful question," he said. "What do you think?"

"I think you will win the war," I said. "I don't know how, but I think you'll find a way to meld the new with the old and retain the beautiful peace that pervades the kingdom."

"That will not be easy," the chief justice said. "But we are trying."

Chapter 18

FOR THE LOVE OF THE GAME

IT WAS EIGHT P.M. and I was at home in the living room sitting on a couch. Carrie was out to dinner with some friends. Claudia and Dechen, our nanny/babysitter, were asleep in Claudia's bedroom.

Ring. Uh-oh! As I looked at the phone, I couldn't help but remember that unpleasant call from Sonam Kesang a couple of months ago. I thought of that call every time the phone rang.

I picked up the receiver. "Hello?"

Silence for a moment. Then a little boy's voice spoke. "Sir, hello," he said sheepishly. "My name is Rinchen."

Huh? Who was that? Somebody from my clinics? This was very odd. Maybe something was wrong? Why was some stranger of a little boy calling me?

"Coach," Rinchen said. Ah-ha! Must be a golfer. He continued, "I have never golfed. I never went to your clinics. But my friends, they go, and I always want to come. But my schoolwork."

I said nothing. The boy was now speaking a million miles a minute. He was clearly nervous.

"Coach, I would like to play in the Bhutan Junior Open tomorrow," Rinchen said. "My friends tell me it will be much fun."

"You've never played golf?" I said.

"No, but I love to learn to play," Rinchen said, his voice a bit calmer. "Can I join the youth program?"

This was wonderful and bold. To children, I must have been considered like a *dasho*—in other words, a pretty important person. That's because anybody who hangs around with the Royal Thimphu members seems important to Bhutanese kids. So for Rinchen to have tracked down my phone number and called me out of the blue took amazing bravery. I'm sure he sat by the phone debating whether to call me, just because it would not be proper social etiquette for a Bhutanese boy to call a dasho he'd never met.

I was so impressed that I wanted Rinchen to come and play in the tournament.

"Please, come to the golf course at seven-thirty," I said. "We'd love to include you in the tournament."

THE BHUTAN JUNIOR Open was another crazy idea of mine. So many of the kids at my clinics were playing so well and so many were coming to practice with me every afternoon from Monday to Friday on the big field at Changlimithang soccer stadium in downtown Thimphu, I decided the kids deserved a big tournament. It would celebrate the great strides they'd made in golf and their dedication over the past couple of months, and it would be a good-bye gift from me.

My first stop was Lyonpo Khandu Wangchuk, the foreign minister and president of both the Bhutan Golf Federation and Royal Thimphu. He graciously said I could have Royal Thimphu for an entire Sunday morning. Some members weren't too happy, seeing that they wouldn't be able to play their routine

Sunday morning games, but there was nothing they could do. When Lyonpo Khandu speaks at Royal Thimphu, everybody listens. No questions asked.

I then recruited some club members to volunteer. A dozen men and Camilla Bang, the Danish woman who'd been on my trek to Jhomolhari, agreed to work with me.

Next, I invited sixty children—boys and girls ages four to eighteen. I divided them into six divisions, by a combination of skill level and age, with a boys and a girls group in each division. The best players would play nine regulation holes, while the less skilled kids would play four modified short holes. The volunteers would follow the groups to be sure the kids played by the rules and counted every stroke. I used a ruler and a pen to create a special scorecard for the event and made copies at a print shop. I arranged a buffet lunch outside the clubhouse. For prizes, I took the bag of medals I'd brought from home because I'd had a hunch I'd organize some kind of tournament and that finding prizes in Bhutan would be a big chore.

Then something beautiful happened. One afternoon I was on the lesson tee giving a few tips to Dasho Ugyen Tsechup, a brother of the queens, and he was genuinely interested in the tournament—so interested that he offered to buy books and fancy shopping bags so every participant in the Junior Open would get a prize. "I want our children to be readers," Dasho Ugyen Tsechup said. "This will be a start."

WHEN I ARRIVED at Royal Thimphu on the morning of the tournament, it was seven-thirty and the course was empty. So was the parking lot. I guess the restaurant staff was sleeping in that day. As I walked through the small, gravel parking lot and around to the front of the clubhouse, I saw a little boy sitting on the clubhouse steps. His back was facing me. Next to him, there was a blue backpack. He was wearing a gho and black loafers.

When he heard my footsteps, he hurriedly stood up and turned around. He looked me in the eye. "Sir, can I ask a question?" he said.

"Of course," I replied.

"I'm the boy who called you last night," he said. I remembered immediately. How could I forget?

Rinchen continued. "I will play well," he said. "I will not let you down."

The Bhutanese kids probably didn't have such enthusiasm for everything they did, but golf was so new and the possibilities probably seemed endless. I imagined many of the kids dreamed that through golf they, too, might become a big-shot dasho, maybe even a lyonpo.

THE TOURNAMENT WENT off without a hitch. By eight-thirty, all sixty children were in their respective playing groups, ranging from threesomes to fivesomes, and most groups had a volunteer chaperone.

I watched the event unfold from the steps of the clubhouse. It felt damn good to gaze over the course and see it filled with kids and, except for the chaperones, not a single adult. I had lots of friends in Bhutan who were adult golfers, but there was something very satisfying and special about seeing the course filled with youngsters. I felt like my work had been worthwhile. When I arrived a few months ago, virtually no kids played golf. Now lots of them did, and they did so by the rules and with good etiquette.

I watched one little girl, perhaps four feet tall and scrawny as a piece of plywood, with long black hair and a ponytail, whiff three times on the first tee. She smiled and giggled after every whiff. Her fourth shot was a beauty and flew two-thirds of the way to the green. Strangely, she didn't seem too excited. The whiffs, I guess, were more fun.

At about eleven, groups started walking back to the clubhouse after their rounds. The kids sat on the grass with their chaperones and checked and signed their scorecards. I wanted them to learn how tournaments operate and feel that it was a very official event. The scores were surprisingly good. In the top division for boys, the winner shot an even-par 33. In the division for the youngest children (ages four to eight), the winning boy shot 38, as did the winning girl, both over four modified short holes.

The last group back was the second most competitive group, with boys ages twelve to fourteen. They signed their cards, and there was a tie for first; two boys had each shot an eleven-over-par 33 for six regulation holes. I decided to have a sudden-death playoff starting at the first hole, and I recruited all the other kids to stand around the first tee to watch. I was curious to see how the young golfers in the playoff would respond to the pressure of having a gallery.

The first boy, another Rinchen, hit a perfect short iron onto the green. The next boy, Sonam Wangchuk, hit a nice shot, but it landed a few yards short of the green in short grass. The golfers skipped down the fairway toward the green, and the other fifty-eight kids skipped along with them. Watching this made the whole trip worthwhile.

The spectating children formed a circle around the green. They were giggling and chatting, kind of oblivious to the stone-dead serious looks on Rinchen's and Sonam's faces. These kids wanted to win, badly. Sonam hit a low, rolling chip that went 8 feet past the hole. Then Rinchen was in the driver's seat. He was 15 feet from the cup, and it looked like a two-putt would win. His first putt stopped a few inches short of the cup, and he tapped in for par. Sonam read his par putt from both sides of the hole, then crouched behind his ball to get one final read. The putt was dead straight.

He hit it solidly and the ball was heading at the cup, but at the last second it trailed off to the right. Bogey. Rinchen was the winner. But he didn't jump up or dive into the greenside pond. He didn't toss his putter to the sky. He meekly walked over to Sonam, took off his yellow Callaway baseball cap, and shook Sonam's hand.

"Okay," I said, standing in the middle of the green. "Lunch!"

The kids reacted like bulls just released from a pen. They stampeded up the hill toward the clubhouse and wove into the fenced-in grassy area to the side of the clubhouse where the buffet was set up, with white and red rice, mo mos, ema datse, steamed vegetables, and chocolate and vanilla cake. I wondered if the kids had eaten in weeks, they heaped so much food on their plates. But I knew they were not malnourished. They were just thrilled to be eating where the dashos usually eat and devouring food from the very same kitchen that produced the dashos' golfing food.

After lunch, Lyonpo Khandu was the master of ceremonies at the award presentation. I called up every child to receive his or her prize for the day, and each child bowed and shook the special guest's hand as they received their prizes. Lyonpo closed the event with a heartfelt little talk.

"You are the future," he said. "This club will be yours someday. I am an old man." He was joking and said this with a laugh. Lyonpo Khandu was about fifty years old and he was in terrific shape, looking like a fit jogger. He continued, "If you keep working hard and showing dedication, you will soon be winning the big prizes in our big tournaments. I expect that. And who knows what else you can accomplish? The sky is the limit."

AN HOUR LATER, the kids were all gone and the course was chock-full of adults. I was on the little lawn where the buffet and the award ceremony were held. I was alone sitting in a lawn chair.

After three months in this amazing place, I saw that I'd taken the game for granted for a long time. At home I could play or watch pros play whenever I wanted. I worked with many of the most gifted and capable teachers in the game. I had good equipment, and if I wanted to get something else, I could afford to get that, too.

Here, though, every shot with the kids was a little miracle. Best of all, they realized how good they had it. I knew how grateful they were because of their dedication, coming to every clinic on time and with big smiles. The glee the Bhutanese children—and adults—took from playing golf had reignited my appreciation for the game.

I came here to give the Bhutanese a little piece of something I've loved. I took all my knowledge and love of the game, and I teed it up and hit it into the thin air, off above the mountains and the chortens and amid the bustle of Thimphu. I taught people about lag and the line of compression. I had them practicing so hard they were digging holes in bunkers and making burn marks on the practice green. And every shot hit Bhutan and bounced right back at me, cleaner and truer than I'd hit them in the first place.

That's the funny thing about Bhutan. No matter how much you give, the country and its people always give you more in return. There really is something to gross national happiness.

No, Bhutan is not nirvana. They have real problems, just like the rest of the world. But there is some ephemeral sense of peace and happiness the kingdom's denizens exude, individually and collectively. I certainly felt the warmth a couple of days later, during our final night in Bhutan.

We had a constant stream of visitors coming to say au revoir. I'd like to think they were coming to see me, but let's be honest: Claudia had been the big attraction in Bhutan, and she was the center of attention again that night.

At seven-thirty P.M., Kalpana, Benji's live-in maid, entered through the back door, which was propped open. Since that first evening in September when we walked into Benji's house, Kalpana and Claudia had been best buddies, blissfully sharing smiles, burps, and laughs. Now Kalpana was sheepishly standing in our living room holding a box with wrapping paper. Carrie handed Claudia to Kalpana, who held Claudia in one arm and the present in her other arm.

Kalpana sat on a couch and opened the present.

"Whooooeee!" said Carrie, who clapped in appreciation.

Claudia's red cheeks glowed as she smiled. Kalpana lifted a brown teddy bear with red eyes that lit up when you pressed its belly. What a joy to watch, Kalpana and Claudia playing with the teddy bear in a reverie I wished would last forever. A teddy bear would be an average gift to give for many people, but I'm sure it was a splurge for Kalpana, whose monthly salary was about $50—less than what I pay a caddie for a round of golf in New York.

After Kalpana left, a white Land Cruiser pulled up to the

little steel gate at the top of our backyard. The guests were Ly-onpo Ugyen Tshering, the minister of communications; his wife, Patrizia, an Italian; their two children, Ugyen Peljor (a boy), and Lara (his little sister); and their friend Oscar. All three kids had been regulars at my golf clinics. While chatting in the yard, Lara rushed over to me and opened her mouth. "Can you tell what's different?" she said.

One of her upper front teeth was missing. "Was that the loose tooth you showed me a couple of days ago in practice?" I asked.

"Yeah, it fell out this morning," Lara said gleefully.

Back in New York, where life was a perpetual footrace, I often overlooked such delights. But I had learned in Bhutan to appreciate the simple things.

Next, Ugyen Peljor unfurled from his backpack a clear plastic folder with a drawing. "I made it, Coach, for you," he said.

The picture had big blue letters across the top that said *PLAY-ING GOLF IN THE YEAR 2500*, and below that was Ugyen Peljor's rendition of what he thought golf would be like in the fu-ture. As a backdrop in the drawing, he used the New York City skyline with the Empire State Building (labeled as a five-hundred-year-old monument) and flying taxis, and below that there was a golf scene that included hovercarts, an auto caddie (a machine on wheels that carries clubs), a club testing robot to help with club se-lection, and what he called an "animatronic automatic golf robot."

As Ugyen Peljor held the drawing in the plastic in front of me, he read aloud the inscription he'd written on the side of it:

TO RICK

FROM UGYEN

I'll always remember that you started coaching me in 2002.

After a bunch of sappy hugs, the kids, Patrizia, and Lyonpo Ugyen scampered across our yard toward their SUV. At the top of the hill, Ugyen Peljor stopped. "Let's go give Coach Rick one more hug!" he yelled. The kids barreled back down and wrapped their arms around me. Then Ugyen Peljor, Lara, and Oscar stood side by side holding hands and sang a song they must have written and practiced before coming over:

> We want to thank you, Coach Rick,
> For being our first golf coach
> and showing us how to play golf

Tears all around.

As the kids ran back up the hill, they were giggling and waving good-bye. Lyonpo Ugyen and Patrizia followed them.

Carrie and I, with Claudia in my arms, stood silently. We watched the kids gallop through the little steel door in the fence and hop into the Land Cruiser. Lyonpo Ugyen and Patrizia got into the SUV. The engine started. Ugyen Peljor leaned out a window.

"Good-bye, Coach!" he yelled, waving a hand.

Carrie and I waved back. We didn't say anything.

Chapter 19

GOOD-BYE, BHUTAN

WE WERE GONE, sort of. We were still on Bhutanese soil, but we had gone through customs at the Paro airport and gotten exit stamps in our passports, so legally we were not in the kingdom anymore.

Now we were in the waiting area by the door to the tarmac. There were still twenty minutes until our eleven-twenty A.M. departure. It was a lonely place, this legal no-man's-zone, especially because there was no turning back. Like it or not, we were going home. Or not? In recent e-mails to friends, I had been saying, "We're not coming home soon. We're coming to visit New York for a while."

Outside, there was a steady breeze making the prayer flags on the hillsides flutter. Had the trip been worthwhile? Did I help the Bhutanese learn to play better golf? Would the BYGA succeed? Would the National Assembly enact Carrie's penal code and evidence act? What did the Foreign Ministry officials really think about my Internet columns? Would there ever be a bona fide golf course at the Jhomolhari base camp? Would McDonald's reach Bhutan? Would Claudia remember anything about the trip?

Forty minutes later, my wistful reverie was long gone and

I was excitedly nervous while anticipating the flying experience of my life. One advantage of teaching golf: Pros befriend a terrific cross section of people who they'd probably never otherwise meet. For me, one such person was Druk Air captain Dhendup Gyaltshen. He was an avid golfer who took several lessons and sent one of his sons to my youth clinics. Captain Gyaltshen wasn't flying that day, but he had arranged for me to sit in the cockpit for our sixty-minute flight from Paro to Calcutta, the first leg of our trip to Bangkok. Carrie, of course, was jealous. "Take pictures," she had said as we walked across the tarmac.

So there I was, strapped into the jump seat in back of the cramped cockpit of one of Druk Air's two British Aerospace 146 jets. The captain for this flight was Sangay, and the flight engineer was Kinga. They were doing last-minute preflight checks, reading and clicking the dozens of gauges and controls around them. Their quick work made me nervous; misreading or missetting a gauge by a tiny bit could cause catastrophe. But Sangay, thirty-seven, and Kinga, twenty-seven, were calm and cheerfully chatting as they worked.

Finally Sangay, sitting on the left side of the cockpit, slowly pushed forward the throttles at his side. The engines began to roar, and the jet glided forward.

Sangay turned back to me. "How about a bottle of water?" he said.

My first thought: Shouldn't you be looking forward?

My second thought: I guessed Kinga was steering.

My third thought: I really hoped Kinga was steering.

The cockpit door was open, and a female flight attendant was standing there. "Sure," I replied.

"I'll be right back with the water," the flight attendant said.

Looking at the mountain walls surrounding the airport made me nervous again. How would the plane rise quickly enough to go over the mountains? I had landed twice and taken off once here, but the view from the cockpit was *much* scarier than the view from the passenger cabin.

The terminal was alongside the middle of the runway, so we had to taxi to the end of the runway and turn around to prepare for takeoff. As we taxied, Sangay poured water from a bottle into his plastic cup and blew his nose. I guessed in his relaxed mood it was not a big deal, but maybe it was? Perhaps he should have been checking more gauges? Maybe flying a jet wasn't as hard as it seemed to a novice like me? Perhaps all flight captains are this mellow just before takeoff, while most passengers are biting their fingernails?

"The strobe is on," Kinga said.

"Okay," said Sangay. "I'll make a quick PA."

Sangay welcomed the passengers and wished them a pleasant flight. He then took another sip. "Ahhh," he said. "That's good."

Sangay put the cup down in a plastic holder, and a second later slid his right hand onto the throttles and pushed them forward. The engines roared. We moved forward slowly and then faster, faster, faster. Suddenly, effortlessly, as smoothly as a feather floating in the wind, we were airborne. "Wheels up," said Sangay.

Oh, no! We banked left. Climbing. Climbing. The mountains were straight ahead. We banked right. I looked down and saw a monastery in the middle of the woods. Were the monks playing cards? Making butter sculptures? Did they hear our plane? We banked hard left, then hard right. Death! We were going right at the mountain. The view looked like one of those arcade video games: You either push the throttle and quickly rise, or kaboom!

Fortunately, Sangay kept the throttle pushed and we were still quickly gaining altitude. In a moment we rose above the mountains, and my heart palpitations slowed to a flutter. We were safely cruising through wide-open blue sky.

The view was otherworldy. Snowcapped mountains were off to one side, and I could see Jhomolhari and its neighbor Jichu Drakye, which is shaped like a triangle. Looking down as we circled back over Paro, the runway and airport looked miniature. The altimeter read 12,500 feet, and it was eleven forty-five.

So far, the ride had been bumpy. "Turbulence is common at the lower altitudes," said Kinga. "But it'll smooth out soon." He was right. Five minutes later, we were at 16,400 feet and cruising like a zephyr.

"Okay," Sangay said while cleaning the steering wheel with a Wet-Nap. Strange. Do all pilots clean steering wheels with Wet-Naps? He continued, "We can turn off the seat-belt sign," and Kinga flipped a switch.

Below, signs of life were quickly getting harder to decipher. I could see farms, but not farmers or animals. Monasteries looked like tiny huts. The rivers in the valleys were like sinewy ropes. The snowcapped peaks were visible but behind us, getting smaller and smaller. Bhutan was flying away too fast.

Captain Sangay sipped some water and turned around to talk. His hands were on his lap, not the steering wheel. Again, strange. Should I have been freaking out? Was this standard procedure? I guessed there was nothing for the plane to hit. Or was there? "There's not so much to do now," Sangay said. "Just check a gauge here and there."

I didn't think the passengers would be pleased to see their captain turned around and talking to me. At least Kinga had his hands on a steering wheel, so I guessed we were okay.

It was eleven fifty-five. We were at 24,200 feet. Suddenly a new range of massive mountains appeared to our right. One of the snowy peaks was Kanchenjunga, which straddles the India–Nepal border and is the world's third-tallest summit, at 28,169 feet.

Dazzling is one word to describe the view. But it's hard to capture in words how the view made me feel. Not the mountains; the view in my mind. I was back in our kitchen in Thimphu, sitting at the little wooden table eating red rice and lentils and feeding some to Claudia, who was in her plastic blue baby seat. I was on the practice range at Royal Thimphu, standing across from a pupil while holding a club against the side of his head to keep him steady. I was in the stone hut at Jhomolhari, dancing into the night.

Chill. That was the best way to describe Sangay and Kinga as we cruised through Bhutanese airspace. To them, I guessed this was just another flight. Maybe to them the view wasn't so special anymore; they saw it every day and probably felt like a New York cabbie cruising along Broadway. *Let's just get where we're going, quick!*

By noon we were at 32,000 feet, our cruising altitude, and going 336 nautical miles per hour. "We'd be going faster if we didn't have a 70-knot headwind," Kinga said.

"Why are the Bhutanese so friendly?" I asked.

"It has a lot to do with religion," Captain Sangay said. "Buddhism has compassion, and when you have compassion in your heart you care and try to see people, everybody, as friends."

"Do you see everybody as a friend?" I said.

Captain Sangay smiled. "I try," he said.

Bhutan was fading fast. The mountains behind us were getting smaller and smaller, and the land below was now flat and filled with rice paddies, farms, and enormous rivers snaking through the fields. The air outside was no longer crisp and clear; it was thick and hazy.

"We just crossed into Bangladeshi airspace," Kinga said.

My face was pressed against a window, my eyes were focused on the farmland below. I was remembering my recent talk with the chief justice and our discussion of gross national happiness. He didn't think it was realistic to expect everybody in Bhutan to be happy, but he did think that most of the country's people should be inspired enough to routinely smile. "These are my wishful dreams," the chief justice had said.

I looked at Sangay and Kinga. Each of them was wearing a white button-down pilot shirt, a black necktie, and black slacks. They were silent, staring ahead through the cockpit windows into the hazy blue sky. Sangay and Kinga both had a soft little smile, the same smile a baby has while asleep. The chief justice would be happy.

EPILOGUE

"It's changing so much, so fast, and more is happening every day," said Nima Tshering. He laughed. "In some ways, it is like a new kingdom since you left."

I was speaking by phone to Nima, a friend who I'd given a couple of lessons to at the end of my stay in 2002. He was on his mobile in his office at the Department of Information and Technology in Thimphu. I was on a landline in the den of my apartment in New York City. It was ten-thirty P.M. in Manhattan on January 3, 2007, and nine-thirty A.M. in Thimphu on January 4.

Nima shared some of the mind-jarring changes that have transformed his kingdom since I left. The final draft of the new constitution was completed and readied for enactment in 2008. The fifteen-hundred-megawatt Tala hydroelectric plant opened and, with most of the power being sold to India, helped Bhutan take a huge step in its quest for economic self-sufficiency. Call centers, like those in India, have been planned. The National Assembly enacted Carrie's penal code and evidence act.

Some changes were less grandiose but no less symbolic of progress. A few of the boys in the Bhutan Youth Golf Association got so good at golf, developing low single-digit handicaps, that Royal Thimphu granted them honorary memberships. All of the boys are from poor families, so they are the first hint of golf becoming diversified in the kingdom. And the kids have been taking advantage of their good fortune. They've had several top finishes in the tournaments at Royal Thimphu and won valuable prizes, including Druk Air plane tickets and televisions. In February 2007, three boys were planning to go to Calcutta, India, to play in the Asian Junior Masters and become the first Bhutanese youth to compete in golf outside the country.

But the biggest change, at least to the Bhutanese, occurred on December 9, 2006. The fourth king, Jigme Singye Wangchuck, suddenly and voluntarily abdicated the throne at age fifty-one after thirty-four years in power. The twenty-six-year-old crown prince, Jigme Khesar Namgyal Wangchuck, became the new king. In the original plan to transition the government from a monarchy to a democracy, the fourth king was supposed to abdicate in 2008.

Relinquishing power two years early might not seem earth-shattering to an outsider. But the Bhutanese revered the king like a beloved parent, so his abdication left the kingdom in shock.

During a special meeting attended by his cabinet in the Thimphu dzong on December 14, 2006, the king told the room full of stunned ministers and officials that he had abdicated because it was in the best interest of Bhutan. He said the kingdom was enjoying unprecedented peace, economic prosperity, and modern development, and that he was satisfied that the foundations for the new democracy were firmly in place. He also wanted to give the crown prince and other officials in the new government time to learn how to govern the nation without their most trusted leader. "I have every confidence that there will be unprecedented progress and prosperity for our nation in the reign of our fifth king," said the fourth king.

But the future might not be so rosy. The reign of the fifth king will last for just one year; he will still be the king when Bhutan shifts to democracy in 2008, but his role will be more symbolic because his ruling power will be greatly diminished. That will put Bhutan in uncharted territory. It will be a new democracy sitting amid a sea of countries in which experiments with democracy have been modestly successful, at best. Will Bhutan become a land of Maoist uprisings, corruption, and environmental desecration, like its neighbor Nepal? Will Bhutan be prone to government coups, as happened in Thailand in 2006? Or will democracy succeed and gross national happiness prevail, providing even greater peace, prosperity, and stability for Bhutan?

As Nima told me, the scary thing for Bhutan is that nobody knows the answers to those questions. "Only time will tell," Nima said.

ACKNOWLEDGMENTS

Kadinchey (pronounced "ka-din-chey"). That's "thank you" in Dzongkha, and I owe sincere thanks to the Kingdom of Bhutan and its people. The Bhutanese have showered smiles, warmth, and brotherly love—gross national happiness, you could say—on my family and me since our first contact with the kingdom in 2000.

Some of the people in Bhutan to whom I owe special kadincheys for their beautiful help while we've been in Bhutan and while working on this book are: Sonam Kesang, Benji, Tobgye, Genzing, the chief justice, Lyonpo Khandu Wangchuk, Patrizia, Habu, Lyonpo Ugyen Tshering, Buddha, Marta, Shanti, Kalpana, Francoise Pommaret, Tashi Namgay, Palden, Fritz, Father Kinley, Nima, Yougs, Norzom, and Tashi.

I am also deeply grateful to Karma Lam Dorji, who since 2002 has devoted himself to making the Bhutan Youth Golf Association a success; to all of the children in the BYGA; and to the American golf pros, past and present, who've trekked to Bhutan to work as golfing missionaries with the BYGA. All of you have given me more than I could ever give you.

Major kadincheys also go to Carrie, my wife. During that bizarre autumn day at Royal Thimphu in October 2000 when Sonam Kesang asked me if I wanted to become Bhutan's first golf pro, Carrie told me to accept the job, and without her crucial blessing the adventure that became this book would not have unfolded. Carrie has also blessed me, and this book, with her savvy editing and guidance. Claudia, our daughter, deserves loving thanks for embracing her Himalayan jaunts with gusto and joy. (Ricky, our son, also was a gleeful Marco Polo in diapers during his first Himalayan voyage.)

As for this book, it exists in no small part because of the vision of my former agent, Rob Robertson; my current agent, Laura Dail, whose omnipresent smile, brilliant ideas, and deft editing have been blessings nonpareil; and Kathy Belden, my supremely smart and kindhearted editor at Bloomsbury. Kadinchey to all of you for putting up with my little deadline delays. Sorry, I was just being Bhutanese.

Finally, thank you Mom and Gram. And for Dad, Linda, and Maria: I thank you deeply for babysitting and giving me time to write.

Several books and Web sites provided invaluable research material. They include the *Lonely Planet Bhutan* guidebook; *Kuensel* and the *Bhutan Times*, the Bhutanese newspapers; *Bhutan: The Dragon Kingdom in Crisis*, by Nari Rustomji; *Gross National Happiness and Development*, edited by Karma Ura and Karma Galay; *The Jesuit and the Dragon*, by Howard Solverson; kuzuzangpo.com, the Web blog; and several Bhutanese government Web sites.

Last but not least, thanks to everybody at *Sports Illustrated* for giving me the opportunity to complete this project.

A NOTE ON THE AUTHOR

RICK LIPSEY is a writer-reporter at *Sports Illustrated*, and he cowrote *In Every Kid There Lurks a Tiger* with Rudy Duran. His work has also appeared in *Golf*, *Golf Illustrated*, *Golf Pro*, the *Christian Science Monitor*, the *New York Times*, and the *Wall Street Journal*. He lives in New York City.

While living in Bhutan, Lipsey started the Bhutan Youth Golf Association, a year-round program that he continues to manage from New York. The BYGA, a registered charity in the United States, provides daily clinics, tournaments, educational field trips, and academic scholarships to Bhutanese boys and girls ages four to eighteen. Lipsey also leads exclusive cultural and trekking tours to Bhutan as a means of supporting the BYGA. His Web site is www.golfbhutan.com.